JB JOSSEY-BASS

Have Fun with the
PRESIDENTS

Activities, Projects, and Fascinating Facts

David C. King

BICENTENNIAL
1807
WILEY
2007
BICENTENNIAL

John Wiley & Sons, Inc.

To my lovely wife, Sharon

Published by Jossey-Bass
A Wiley Imprint
989 Market Street, San Francisco, CA 94103-1741
www.josseybass.com

Illustrations © 2007 by JT Morrow

Design and composition by Navta Associates, Inc.

Jossey-Bass books and products are available through most bookstores. To contact Jossey-Bass directly call our Customer Care Department within the U.S. at 800-956-7739, outside the U.S. at 317-572-3986, or fax 317-572-4002.

Jossey-Bass also publishes its books in a variety of electronic formats. Some content that appears in print may not be available in electronic books.

Library of Congress Cataloging-in-Publication Data

King, David C.
    Have fun with the presidents : activities, projects, and fascinating facts / David C. King. — 1st ed.
      p. cm.
    Includes index.
    ISBN-13: 978-0-471-67905-9 (paper)
  1. Presidents—United States—Bibliography—Juvenile literature. 2. Presidents—United States—Miscellanea—Juvenile literature. 3. Presidents—Study and teaching—Activity programs—United States. 4. Creative activities and seat work—Juvenile literature. I. Title.
    E176.1.K475 2007
    973.09'9—dc22   2006023905

Printed in the United States of America

10 9 8 7 6 5 4 3 2 1

CONTENTS

INTRODUCTION

Who are the forty-two men who have been the presidents of the United States? What personal qualities have they had in common? In what ways have they been more different than alike? Throughout this book you'll find many of the ways the presidents have been alike. Many have served in the military, for example. In fact, a few were great generals before they became president, including George Washington, Andrew Jackson, Ulysses S. Grant, and Dwight D. Eisenhower. And yet the men who led the country through its major wars were never battlefield leaders. That includes Abraham Lincoln (Civil War), Woodrow Wilson (World War I), and Franklin D. Roosevelt (World War II).

You'll also find that the family life of our presidents shows more differences than similarities. Most have had children, for example, but the number of offspring varies considerably. John Tyler, our tenth president, holds the record. He had eight children with his first wife and seven with his second. He was seventy years old when his fifteenth child was born. By contrast, George and Martha Washington had no children of their own (Martha had two by a previous marriage), and James Buchanan, a lifetime bachelor, also had none.

Many first ladies have stayed in the background. First Lady Jane Pierce, recovering from a family tragedy, was not seen in public for two full years. Others, such as Eleanor Roosevelt and Hillary Rodham Clinton, were very active in the affairs of the nation. And Edith Wilson, wife of Woodrow Wilson, the twenty-eighth president, was called Madame President because she made nearly all the decisions during the president's slow recovery from a stroke that he suffered late in his second term.

Our presidents have even shown sharp differences in their reactions to the experience of being president. Some have enjoyed the office. For example, Theodore Roosevelt told a reporter, "I will confess to you confidentially that I like the job." Ulysses S. Grant, who suffered through political scandals during his two terms, still enjoyed being president and remained immensely popular long after he left office. Others, such as Benjamin Harrison, were happy to retire.

Throughout these pages, you'll encounter lots of intriguing and little-known facts about the presidents, their families, and the times in which they lived. You can even make up your own game of presidential trivia: Which presidential couple spoke Chinese in the White House as a way of maintaining their privacy? How many presidents were Civil War generals? What presidential children managed to sneak a pony into a White House elevator so that they could take it to their sick brother's bedroom? And which president had broccoli banned from the White House kitchen?

Have Fun with the Presidents is far more than a book of facts. You'll discover that there are lots of games and puzzles, each of which is connected to a president, such as a word scramble about Franklin D. Roosevelt and a game of battlefield strategy in the President Grant chapter. You'll also find activities related to a presidency, such as decorating Easter eggs to honor First Lady Lucy Hayes, who started the first Easter Egg Roll on the White House lawn in 1878. And there are many presidential recipes, including Dwight D. Eisenhower's favorite dessert or Texas Hash to honor George W. Bush. Above all else, this book is about having fun while you learn about America's presidents.

George Washington

First President, 1789–1797

Born *February 22, 1732, Westmoreland County, Virginia*
Died *December 14, 1799, Mount Vernon, Virginia*

When George Washington took the oath of office as the nation's first president, no one knew what to expect. After all, the Americans had invented a new form of government with a new position of leadership. As Washington himself said about his new job, "I walk on untrodden ground."

One thing was certain: no one could imagine anyone better than Washington to take on this crucial task. For years, the American people had become accustomed to turning to Washington to lead them through hard times.

He was a tall, rugged, commanding figure. He had spent much of his life outdoors and was an expert horseman. In his youth, he had worked as a surveyor, measuring land and marking boundaries over large areas of Virginia. Throughout his military career, he had always shown great calm in battle. In his first real battle, at the start of the French and Indian War, he had been riding with British troops when the column was ambushed by Indian warriors and French troops. The twenty-three-year-old Washington had two horses shot from under him and four bullet holes through his coat, but he still managed to lead the survivors to safety.

In 1775, following the first fighting of the American Revolution, the Continental Congress called on Washington to create and lead a Continental army to fight for America's freedom. His inspired leadership was the key ingredient in winning independence from Great Britain.

As president, Washington never had it easy. He had to find a balance between advisers who were pushing him to take the new country in different directions. He also managed to steer a middle course in dealing with other countries, especially when war broke out between the French and the English.

Washington's life in retirement was brief. Trapped in a snowstorm while riding on his Mount Vernon estate in Virginia, he became ill and died two days later.

☆☆☆☆☆☆☆☆☆☆☆
Family Matters

Washington became known as the Father of His Country because he was such a great leader, both in the army and as the first president. His wife, Martha, could be said to be the Mother of Her Country. During the Revolutionary War, she traveled the countryside with her own fruit pies for the troops. George and Martha had no children of their own, but Martha had a son and a daughter from a previous marriage whom George helped raise as his own.

☆☆☆☆☆☆☆☆☆☆☆

Dear Mr. ?

At the time of Washington's election, no one knew how to address the nation's chief executive. Many wanted him to have a title like the royalty of Europe, such as Your Elective Majesty, or Your Highness, the President. (In fact, many thought Washington would soon become king or emperor.) Washington preferred the simple title of Mr. President, and that became permanent.

Washington Cherry Pie

Things You'll Need

2 ready-made 9-inch pie
    crusts

1 quart pitted cherries, sour
    if possible (frozen or canned
    work well)

⅛ teaspoon salt

1 cup sugar (¾ cup for sweet
    cherries)

1 tablespoon all-purpose
    flour

adult helper

9-inch pie tin

small mixing bowl

wooden spoon

table knife

aluminum foil

oven mitts

cooling rack

measuring cup

measuring spoon

MAKES 6 SERVINGS

Many legends and myths have been told about Washington, but none is more well known than the one about the boy George cutting down a cherry tree, then confessing to his father with the words "I cannot tell a lie."

In honor of the myth, here is one of the oldest recipes for cherry pie (with the modern adaptation of ready-made pie crust).

1 Have an adult preheat the oven to 450 degrees F.

2 Roll out the dough into thin circles and line the pie tin with one crust.

3 Pour the cherries into the pie tin and spread evenly with a spoon.

4 Mix the salt, sugar, and flour together in a small mixing bowl. Sprinkle this mixture over the cherries.

5 Use a table knife to cut the second pie crust into strips about three-quarters of an inch wide. Make a latticework of these for a top crust by crisscrossing the strips.

6 Fit strips of aluminum foil around the edges of the pie tin to hold in the juices.

7 Have an adult wearing oven mitts put the pie in the oven. Bake at 450 degrees F for up to 40 minutes or until the top crust is golden brown. Use oven mitts to remove the pie and cool on a rack. Cut and serve when the pie is cool (at least room temperature).

Washington

Things named in honor of Washington include Washington State (the only state named after a president); Washington, D.C.; Washington College (now Washington and Lee); the USS *George Washington*, the first ballistic missile submarine; plus 33 counties, 120 towns, 7 mountains, 8 streams, 10 lakes, and 9 colleges, as well as the George Washington Bridge and the Washington Monument.

Build a Word

Use the clues to find nine words associated with George Washington. Write your answers in the spaces. The letters in the boxes will form a tenth word. Unscramble the letters to find a word that describes Washington.

1 Washington's military title

1 _ ⬚ _ _ _ _ _

2 Name of the family estate

2 _ _ _ ⬚ _ _ _ _ _ _

3 Washington was commander of Virginia's _____.

3 _ _ _ ⬚ _ _ _

4 French ally against Great Britain

4 _ _ ⬚ _ _ _ _

5 Before his presidency, he worked as a _____.

5 ⬚ _ _ _ _ _ _ _

6 He was always calm in _____.

6 _ _ _ _ _ ⬚

7 The army he commanded

7 _ _ ⬚ _ _ _ _ _ _

8 The War for Independence

8 ⬚ _ _ _ _ _ _ _ _

9 Victory over England gave America _____.

9 _ _ _ ⬚ _ _ _ _ _

10 _ _ _ _ _ _ _ _ _

Answers appear at the back of the book.

Observe good faith and justice toward all nations. Cultivate peace and harmony with all.

5

John ★ Adams

Second President, 1797–1801

Born *October 30, 1735, Braintree (now Quincy), Massachusetts*
Died *July 4, 1826, Quincy, Massachusetts*

John Adams did not enjoy his role as either Washington's vice president or as president. Part of the problem was that he was too proud and stubborn to give in to the demands of politics. As a result, he lost the support of Congress and many of the American people.

Adams deserved a better fate. As a Massachusetts lawyer, he had been one of the early leaders of the struggle for independence. He served in the Continental Congress during the critical years of the struggle (1774–1778) and was on the committee to draft the Declaration of Independence. He represented the new nation in France and later in England. In France, he helped negotiate the alliance that brought the powerful French into the War for Independence. Later, he helped to negotiate the peace treaty with England.

When George Washington was elected president, Adams was elected the country's first vice president. The vice presidency, he wrote, "is the most insignificant office that ever the invention of man contrived." In 1796, when Washington refused to consider a third term, Adams was elected the nation's second president.

Europe in those years was locked in the first of a long series of wars between England and France. Alexander Hamilton, the secretary of the Treasury, wanted Adams to declare war on France if necessary. Adams did build up a strong navy, but he avoided war. He also supported the Alien and Sedition Acts designed to stop opposition to the government. These laws outraged Thomas Jefferson, the secretary of state. Opposition from both Hamilton's and Jefferson's supporters cost Adams any chance for reelection in 1800.

During his long retirement, Adams made peace with Jefferson, and the two engaged in a long and remarkable correspondence. Both men died on July 4, 1826—the fiftieth anniversary of the Declaration of Independence.

The White House

Adams and his wife, Abigail, moved into the still-unfinished President's House (later, the White House). On their second night there, Adams wrote, "I pray Heaven to bestow the best Blessings on the House and all that shall hereafter inhabit it. May none but honest and wise men ever rule beneath this roof."

Cool Berry Flummery

Like many of the nation's founders, Adams was fond of good food, and the leading families of Philadelphia often lavished eight-course meals on the men of the Continental Congress. Desserts were often sweet but light, like this berry flummery, which was John Adams's favorite.

1 Have an adult use a paring knife to hull and cut up the strawberries. Rinse the berries in a colander or strainer under cold running water.

2 Pour ¾ cup water into the saucepan and add the berries. Cover and cook over medium heat until the berries are soft, about 10 minutes. Stir occasionally with a wooden spoon, and lower the heat if the berries begin to stick.

3 Put the sugar, salt, and cornstarch into a bowl and mix with a teaspoon or fork.

4 Stir the sugar-cornstarch mixture into the berries and mix well with a wooden spoon. Reduce the heat to low, and continue cooking over low heat until the mixture thickens, about 10 minutes.

5 Turn off the heat and let the mixture cool for a few minutes, then spoon it into dessert dishes and chill for at least an hour before serving. Top with whipped cream or ice cream if you wish.

Things You'll Need

3–4 cups strawberries or raspberries

3/4 cup water

1 cup sugar

¼–½ teaspoon salt

6 tablespoons cornstarch

whipped cream or vanilla ice cream (optional)

adult helper

paring knife

measuring cup

measuring spoon

colander or strainer

medium-size saucepan and lid

wooden spoon

small bowl

teaspoon or fork

6 small dessert dishes

MAKES 6 SERVINGS

☆ ☆

Family Matters

First Lady Abigail Adams was a thoughtful and energetic partner. She managed their farm and law practice during the more than twenty years that John was away on the country's business. When he was at the Constitutional Convention in Philadelphia, she wrote to urge him and his colleagues to "remember the ladies," by granting them basic rights in the Constitution, including the right to vote. John and Abigail had five children, including John Quincy Adams, who became the sixth U.S. president.

☆ ☆

Fourth of July Celebration Invitation

© 2007 by John Wiley & Sons, Inc.

John Adams believed that Independence Day—the birthday of the nation—should be celebrated with "games, sports, guns, bells, bonfires, and illuminations." This tradition has continued with July 4th picnics, music, and fireworks. Although paper was scarce in colonial times, decorative paper cuts were used for invitations. You can use your paper cuts for an invitation to a Fourth of July celebration.

1 Decide how many invitations you'll need. Use white paper for the cards; make half the paper cuts red and half blue. You can make 3 or 4 designs on each sheet of construction paper.

2 Make copies of the patterns and cut them out.

3 Fold a piece of red or blue construction paper in half and tape one of the patterns to the paper. Be sure the dotted line is on the fold.

4 Cut around the paper pattern *and* through both layers of construction paper except at the fold line. Remove the tape and the pattern.

5 Unfold the design and lay it flat on a piece of white paper. Glue it in place. Write the details of your celebration (date, time, etc.) on the invitation.

6 Repeat for as many invitations as you need, alternating red and blue on white paper cards.

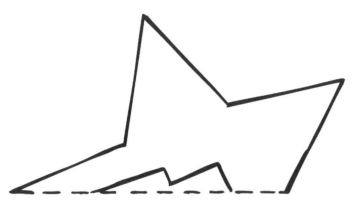

Lay this edge along the fold.

Lay this edge along the fold.

Modesty is a virtue that can never thrive in public. . . . A man must be his own trumpeter.

THOMAS
JEFFERSON

Third President, 1801–1809

Born *April 13, 1743, Albemarle County, Virginia*
Died *July 4, 1826, Monticello, Virginia*

odern scholars agree that Thomas Jefferson had the most brilliant mind of any president. His curiosity and his talents led him in many directions. A self-taught architect, he designed some of the most beautiful buildings in America, including his home, Monticello. He had considerable knowledge of law, science, philosophy, math, and six or seven languages. He was also an inventor and a talented musician. And although he was considered a poor public speaker, he was a brilliant writer who was responsible for penning the Declaration of Independence.

A tall, handsome man with red-brown hair and a friendly manner, he gained attention early in the struggle for independence with the keen logic of his arguments. After the American Revolution, Jefferson went on to serve as a diplomat to France, then as George Washington's secretary of state. In 1796, he was elected vice president to John Adams and then president in 1800.

As president, Jefferson brought a new simplicity to the office. Fancy carriages and elegant parties were gone. He reduced the army and the navy, and emphasized the need for as little government interference in people's affairs as possible.

He believed in a strict interpretation of the Constitution, and that presented him with a dilemma. In 1803, when he sought to buy the port of New Orleans from France, Napoléon Bonaparte, the French leader, offered to sell not only New Orleans but the entire Louisiana Territory for a mere $15 million. The deal was too good to pass up, but the Constitution said nothing about adding new lands. After wrestling with the issue, Jefferson and most members of Congress approved the Louisiana Purchase. Jefferson had always believed that the nation's future greatness lay west of the Mississippi River. The Louisiana Purchase clearly pointed America in that direction.

The Slavery Issue

Some modern writers are critical of Jefferson and other founders for speaking of liberty and equality while continuing to own slaves. Jefferson wrestled with this matter throughout his life. Slaves were a major investment, and to free them would create financial disaster for his family. He worked to achieve a gradual emancipation (freeing) of all slaves. In 1783, he drew up a proposal for outlawing slavery in the lands of the Northwest Territory. This became the first national law limiting slavery.

Family Matters

Jefferson's wife, Martha, shared his love of music. He often accompanied her on the violin when she sang. They were very close during their ten-year marriage, and they had five daughters and a son. Jefferson was devastated when Martha died in 1782, and he vowed never to remarry. During his presidency, the duties of first lady were performed by Dolley Madison, the wife of Jefferson's secretary of state James Madison, who became the fourth president of the United States.

9

In 1808, Jefferson refused to consider a third term, following the two-term model established by Washington. The precedent of the two-term presidency remained for more than a century. After his presidency, Jefferson enjoyed a long retirement, writing thousands of letters and receiving a steady stream of visitors. On July 4, 1826, the fiftieth anniversary of the Declaration of Independence, both he and John Adams died.

Fossil Imprints

Things You'll Need

several sheets of newspaper
2 cups all-purpose flour
½ cup salt
¾ cup water
measuring cup
mixing bowl
spoon
objects for making imprints

Jefferson was fascinated by fossils of ancient life-forms, including dinosaurs. He collected crates of fossils from limestone deposits around Monticello. In addition, the Lewis and Clark expedition that was sent to explore the Louisiana Territory brought back fossils and plaster casts of fossils.

In this activity, you can use common items, such as seashells, leaves, stones, and even real fossils to make plaster imprints.

1 Spread several sheets of newspaper on your work surface.

2 Put the flour, salt, and water in a mixing bowl. Stir to blend. When the mixture becomes thick, knead it with your hands.

3 Form the salt dough into 4 or 5 round balls. Flatten each ball with the palm of your hand.

4 Use different objects to make impressions in the salt dough. Let your imprints dry for a few days, then put them on display.

Do the Numbers

History books often point out that the Louisiana Purchase doubled the size of the United States. In this activity, you'll calculate how much new land was added. The following states and territories existed before the purchase. The area of each is also listed.

Jefferson the Inventor

Jefferson's many inventions included the dumbwaiter, the folding chair, the swivel chair, the lazy Susan, and a device for making copies of a letter.

States and Territories before the Louisiana Purchase

Connecticut: 5,000 sq. mi.

Delaware 2,000: sq. mi.

Georgia: 59,000 sq. mi.

Maine: 33,000 sq. mi.

Maryland: 10,500 sq. mi.

Massachusetts: 8,000 sq. mi.

New Hampshire: 9,000 sq. mi.

New Jersey: 8,000 sq. mi.

New York: 49,000 sq. mi.

North Carolina: 52,500 sq. mi.

Ohio: 41,000 sq. mi.

Pennsylvania: 45,000 sq. mi.

Rhode Island: 1,000 sq. mi.

South Carolina: 31,000 sq. mi.

Tennessee: 42,000 sq. mi.

Vermont: 9,500 sq. mi.

Virginia: 40,500 sq. mi.

West Virginia: 24,000 sq. mi.

Northwest Territory: 200,000 sq. mi.

Michigan Territory: 58,000 sq. mi.

Mississippi Territory: 47,000 sq. mi.

The Louisiana Purchase

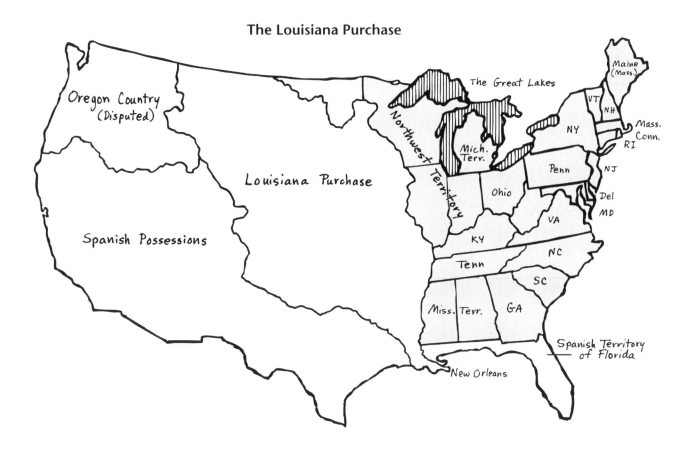

The Louisiana Territory was 828,000 square miles in area. How does that compare to the area of the 18 states plus Michigan, Mississippi, and the Northwest territories?

1 Add up the total area of the 18 states and 3 territories; the total is _____ square miles.

2 Which was larger, the Louisiana Territory or all of the existing states and territories combined? _____ By how much? _____

3 What was the total area of the United States after the purchase? _____

Answers appear at the back of the book.

I have sworn on the altar of God eternal hostility against every form of tyranny of the mind of man.

JAMES MADISON

Fourth President, 1809–1817

Born *March 16, 1751, Port Conway, Virginia*
Died *June 28, 1836, Montpelier Station, Virginia*

☆☆☆☆☆☆☆☆☆☆

Family Matters

In 1794, Madison married "Dolley" Payne Todd, a young widow. At age forty-three, he was sixteen years older than Dolley. She was attractive and outgoing, the center of attention at every social gathering. Dolley Madison served as first lady longer than any other woman. She often performed this role during Thomas Jefferson's eight years as president, as well as her husband's eight.

☆☆☆☆☆☆☆☆☆☆

The President in Battle

In August 1814, British troops invaded south of Washington, D.C., and marched on the nation's capital. The Madisons were about to sit down to dinner when the news came. Madison rushed off to join the American defenders, becoming the only president to lead troops in battle while in office. But the battle was a disaster, and the president and the Americans fled from the British.

Dolley Madison waited for the president's return before she fled the White House as the British approached. When household staff could not get a favorite full-length portrait of George Washington off the wall, she ordered them to cut it from the frame, rolled it up, and carried it in her escape. The invaders enjoyed the Madisons' meal, then torched the building.

James Madison has the distinction of being the smallest president. He stood 5 feet 4 inches tall and weighed about 100 pounds. He may have been small in physical stature, but he is considered one of the giants among the nation's founders. One of the delegates to the Constitutional Convention in 1787 commented, "Every person seems to acknowledge his greatness. . . . In the management of every question, [Madison] took the lead."

In frail health as a child, he remained thin and sickly throughout his life. He was taught at home until he was eighteen, when he entered Princeton, where he was known as a brilliant scholar, often studying sixteen hours a day.

During the American Revolution, Madison was a member of the Continental Congress. In 1787, he was the chief recorder for the Constitutional Convention in Philadelphia. Much of what we know of those historic deliberations comes from his detailed notes. He also played a vital role in the struggle to have the Constitution ratified, and he is often called the Father of the Constitution. Madison was elected to the House of Representatives in 1789, where he helped draft the Bill of Rights (the first ten amendments to the Constitution).

After serving as Thomas Jefferson's secretary of state for eight years, he was elected president in 1808 and reelected in 1812. His administration was caught in the continuing wars between Great Britain and Napoléon Bonaparte's France. The warships of both nations frequently captured American ships to keep them from trading with the enemy, but the British caused greater anger with the practice of impressing American seamen—claiming the men were really British subjects and forcing them to serve in the Royal Navy. In Congress, a vocal group called the War Hawks demanded a declaration of war against Great Britain. Their real goal was to use the war to take Canada from Britain and Florida from Spain.

Madison finally agreed, and the country fought its second war against Great Britain. The War of 1812 was a near disaster for the United States, although the U.S. Navy covered itself with glory. The Americans managed to avoid total defeat and won the final battles of the war. A peace treaty was signed late in 1814. Madison retired to his Virginia estate in 1817, where he died in 1836.

The Art of Fresco

The Madisons oversaw the restoration of the White House after it was burned by the British. One of the many artistic techniques used was *fresco,* which means "fresh," referring to the technique of painting on wet plaster. The paint becomes part of the plaster as it dries. You can make a modified version as a colorful wall hanging.

Things You'll Need

sheet of white paper
pencil
several sheets of newspaper
box of plaster of paris (available at craft and hardware stores)
disposable plastic or paper pail for mixing
strong paper plate
stir stick
paintbrush
water color or tempera paints—any colors
6-inch piece of yarn or twine

1 Use paper and pencil to draw a design for your fresco in a circle about the size of the paper plate.

2 Spread several sheets of newspaper on your work surface. Mix the plaster of paris in the pail according to the directions on the box.

3 Pour the plaster into the paper plate, smoothing the surface with the stir stick. While the plaster is still wet, poke a hole through what will be the top of the hanging.

4 Paint your picture on the plaster while it is still damp.

5 Let the plaster dry, then remove it from the paper plate.

6 Push yarn or twine through the hole and tie it in a double knot. Your fresco is ready to hang on a wall in your room.

Long Live the President!

Most early Americans didn't live very long, but interestingly many presidents did. James Madison, for example, was eighty-five when he died.

Listed below are the ages achieved by some of our early presidents. Use the dates in this book at the beginning of each chapter to match the president to the age. (Madison is done for you.)

1 Age 73 _____

2 Age 85 _____ *James Madison* _____

3 Age 78 _____

4 Age 80 _____

5 Age 68 _____

6 Age 91 _____

7 Age 81 _____

8 Age 83 _____

9 Age 67 _____

10 Age 72 _____

Answers appear at the back of the book.

In Their Own

The happy union of these states is a wonder; their constitution is a miracle; their example the hope of liberty throughout the world.

13

JAMES MONROE

Fifth President, 1817–1825

Born *April 28, 1758, Westmoreland County, Virginia*
Died *July 4, 1831, New York City, New York*

ew presidents have had the good fortune to preside over such a period of calm, peace, and growth as James Monroe, and Monroe had the right personality for the times. Tall and husky, he had a quiet dignity to which people warmed. He became the first president to tour the country, traveling from Maine to what was then the western frontier town of Detroit. He was cheered everywhere, and a Boston newspaper declared that this was "the Era of Good Feeling." The label stuck.

Monroe was the last of the Revolution-era leaders to become president. As a young man, he studied law under Thomas Jefferson, and the two became close friends. In his teens, he served in the Continental Army under Washington. At age twenty-four, he was elected to the Virginia legislature. Monroe was elected senator and then governor of Virginia. Following a period as minister to France, he became secretary of state under James Madison.

The nation grew vigorously during Monroe's presidency. Five new states entered the Union, including Missouri, the first state west of the Mississippi, and Florida, which was purchased from Spain. Monroe was reelected in 1820 with every electoral vote but one. (Each state has as many electoral votes as it has members of Congress. The candidate with the most electoral votes is elected.) The dissenting vote was cast by an elector who believed only Washington should have the honor of a unanimous election.

In the 1820s, the people of Latin America were fighting wars of independence against Spain, and Monroe's administration had to decide where the United States would stand. The Spanish government asked France and other European countries to help it regain its colonial empire. In 1823, Monroe issued a statement warning that "the American continents," including both North and South America, were to remain "free and independent" of any European influence. This statement, known as the Monroe Doctrine, has been a cornerstone of American foreign policy ever since.

After his two terms as president, Monroe retired to his Virginia home. Financial problems forced him to sell his property in 1826. He lived with his daughter in New York City until his death in 1831—the third of the first five presidents to die on the Fourth of July. (Adams and Jefferson had both died on July 4, 1826.)

☆☆☆☆☆☆☆☆☆☆☆

Family Matters

Monroe and his wife, Elizabeth, were an elegant-looking couple. Elizabeth, however, suffered from a chronic illness and often could not attend White House functions. Their oldest daughter, Eliza, filled in for her. Another daughter, Maria, was the first president's daughter to be married in the White House. Their only son, James, died in infancy.

☆☆☆☆☆☆☆☆☆☆☆

Word Search

This puzzle contains nine words or names associated with the presidency of James Monroe. When you find one of the words or names, draw a line around it. One is done for you. Notice that a word or name can go in any direction: left to right; right to left; up, down, or on a diagonal.

Here are the words to look for:

DOCTRINE	ERA	LATIN
ELECTORAL	GOOD	AMERICA
ELIZABETH	FEELING	MADISON

```
T  R  V  O  T  G  M  B  R  L  A  G
R  H  N  L  O  W  E  D  A  S  L  N
M  T  I  O  T  I  N  T  I  R  Y  I
A  E  D  F  A  R  I  E  T  A  L  L
E  B  A  M  D  N  R  I  R  I  N  E
F  A  L  A  R  O  T  C  E  L  E  E
T  Z  M  N  L  I  C  G  N  R  N  F
G  I  O  D  T  E  O  M  T  B  C  S
L  L  F  W  R  L  D  R  O  E  F  N
R  E  M  A  D  I  S  O  N  E  D  M
X  M  E  N  A  C  I  R  E  M  A  R
```

Answers appear at the back of the book.

Monroe's Historic Wound

On Christmas night, 1776, General Washington led his battered Continental Army in the famous night crossing of the ice-clogged Delaware River. Their surprise victory in the Battle of Trenton restored the hope of American patriots. Only two Americans were wounded in that stunning victory. One was eighteen-year-old James Monroe, who took a bullet in his shoulder. The bullet remained in his shoulder for the rest of his life.

Jefferson's Imprint

Thomas Jefferson designed Monroe's home near Jefferson's Monticello and supervised construction while Monroe was serving as minister to France. The floor of the patio was made from limestone quarried on the property. The fossilized footprints of dinosaurs are visible in the floor, along with the imprint of a tail and part of a body. (See page 10 for an activity on making a fossil imprint.)

Seminole Patchwork Bookmark

In 1818, President Monroe sent General Andrew Jackson and an army unit into Spanish Florida to stop raids by the Seminole Indians on nearby American settlements. The Seminole managed to escape the army, but Jackson's invasion contributed to Spain's decision to sell Florida to the United States. Some of the Seminole managed to avoid capture by moving deep into the Everglades, where their descendants remain today.

As a tribute to the Seminole, you can make a bookmark using a traditional Seminole patchwork design.

1 On one sheet of construction paper, use a pencil and a ruler to mark a strip 6¼ inches long by 1¼ wide. Repeat this on the second sheet of construction paper. On the third sheet, mark a third strip, but this time only ¾ inch wide.

Things You'll Need

3 sheets of construction paper in 3 colors that go well together

pencil

ruler

scissors

white glue

2 sheets of white paper

piece of lightweight cardboard, about 6 × 8 inches

2 scraps of rickrack—any color

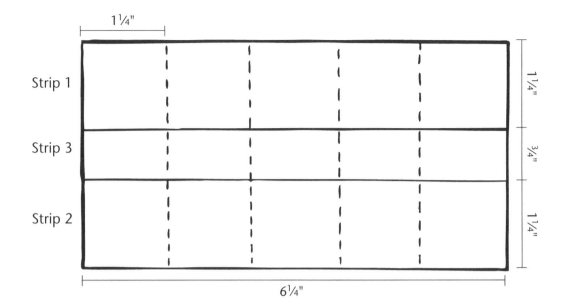

Strip 1

Strip 3

Strip 2

1¼"

1¼"

¾"

1¼"

6¼"

2 Cut out the 3 strips. Glue them to one sheet of white paper, with the narrow strip in the middle.

3 Draw 4 lines across all 3 strips about 1¼ inches apart, as shown in the drawing by the dotted lines. Cut along the dotted lines, creating 5 small strips.

4 Arrange the 5 strips on the second sheet of white paper, tipping the strips at an angle, as shown in the drawing. The top and bottom of the narrow middle strip should line up all the way across. Glue the strips to the white paper.

5 With ruler and pencil, draw a line along each side of the design. Place the lines so that they cut off as little of the side bands as possible. Cut out the design along those pencil lines. The completed design should be about 6¼ inches high and 2 inches wide.

6 Place the patchwork design on the piece of cardboard. Show ½ inch of cardboard at the top and bottom, and ¼ inch on either side. Cut out this cardboard backing and glue the patchwork design to it.

7 Glue a piece of rickrack at the top of the bookmark and another at the bottom. Your Seminole patchwork bookmark is now ready to use or to give as a gift.

In Their Own
WORDS

National honor is national property of the highest value.

John Quincy Adams

Sixth President, 1825–1829

Born *July 11, 1767, Quincy, Massachusetts*
Died *February 23, 1848, Washington, D.C.*

John Quincy Adams was a man of contradictions. Many people considered him cold and unfriendly, for example, but he became the most skilled diplomat of the nation's early years, a position that required great talent in dealing with people. In addition, even though he devoted his life to government service, he always wished he could have been a poet. And although his presidential term was not considered a great success, he followed his term in office with an outstanding career in the House of Representatives.

As a boy growing up near Boston, Adams watched the Battle of Bunker Hill, an event that gave birth to a lifetime of strong patriotism. He spent much of his youth in Europe, where his father, the future president, served as a diplomat to several countries. He became fluent in French, German, Russian, Greek, and Dutch, as well as in English and Latin. In his teens, he also worked as his father's secretary, and later, President Washington sent him on several diplomatic missions.

After a term in the U.S. Senate, Adams became secretary of state for President Monroe. He performed brilliantly in this role, negotiating the purchase of Florida and helping to write the Monroe Doctrine and the Missouri Compromise (which placed limits on the expansion of slavery in new states).

In the presidential election of 1824, when none of the four candidates had a majority of the electoral votes, the House decided the election in Adams's favor. As president, he wanted the government to approve ambitious projects for roads, canals, and a naval academy. But much like his father, he lacked the political skills needed to move Congress, and all of his plans were left for later presidents to achieve.

Adams was defeated in his bid for reelection in 1828. Although deeply disappointed by his loss, Adams did not retire from political life. Instead, he was elected to the House, where he served with distinction for seventeen years. He worked hard to bring an end to slavery and to expand civil rights. In 1848, he collapsed and died in the Speaker's Room of the House of Representatives.

☆☆☆☆☆☆☆☆☆☆

Like Father, Like Son

Both Adams and his father, John Adams, were famous for their brilliant defense work in two high-profile court murder cases. In 1770, John Adams defended the British soldiers accused of murder in the event called the Boston Massacre. In 1841, John Quincy Adams defended the mutineers of a Spanish slave ship, the *Amistad*. Both father and son won stunning victories for the defendants.

☆☆☆☆☆☆☆☆☆☆

Family Matters

Adams met and married his wife, Louisa, in England. She was the only foreign-born first lady. John and Louisa had three sons, George Washington Adams, John Adams II, and Charles Francis Adams, and a daughter who died in infancy. John Adams II was the first president's son to be married in the White House.

© 2007 by John Wiley & Sons, Inc.

½ cup (1 stick) unsalted butter at room temperature
½ cup sugar
1 egg
½ cup all-purpose flour
½ teaspoon nutmeg
nonstick cooking spray or butter for baking sheets
adult helper
measuring cup
measuring spoon
large bowl
wooden spoon and teaspoon
electric mixer (optional)
2 baking sheets
oven mitts
spatula
wire cooling rack
MAKES ABOUT 24 SMALL CAKES

Things You'll Need

sheet of bright-colored construction paper
small spiral notebook
ruler
pencil
scissors
white glue
pen with gold or silver ink

The Mother of Tabloid Journalism

Adams often swam naked in the Potomac River. One afternoon, a journalist, Anne Royall, stole his clothes, agreeing to return them only if the president granted her an interview. He agreed.

Shrewsbury Cakes

First Lady Louisa Adams brought several favorite English recipes to the White House, including this one for a popular English dessert.

1 Have an adult preheat the oven to 350 degrees F.

2 Put the butter in a large bowl, breaking it into smaller pieces with a wooden spoon. Add the sugar and mix with the electric mixer for 3 or 4 minutes until blended. (For a more authentic feel, try blending the sugar and butter by hand with a wooden spoon.)

3 Break the egg into the mixture. Mix again by hand or with the mixer.

4 Stir in the flour and nutmeg. Mix again until the batter is smooth.

5 Spray or butter the baking sheets. Place teaspoons of the batter onto the baking sheets, spacing them about 2 inches apart. Bake for about 10 minutes or until the edges turn brown.

6 Have an adult use oven mitts to remove the baking sheets from the oven. With a spatula, transfer the small cakes to a cooling rack. Cool for 10 or 15 minutes and serve.

Diary

John Quincy Adams kept a careful and detailed diary for sixty-nine years, usually writing in it every day. "There has perhaps not been another individual," he wrote, "whose daily existence has been noted down with his own hand so minutely as mine." You don't have to go as far as Adams did in recording your life, but you are likely to find that a diary is a helpful way to express your thoughts and feelings. Here is an easy way to customize a notebook for a diary.

1 Open the notebook and center it on the construction paper. Use a pencil to trace all the way around the notebook. Use a ruler and a pencil to draw lines about 2 inches from the edges of the notebook.

2 Cut along the outside lines. Cut the corners of the construction paper as shown in the drawing. Cut 2 small pieces from the center of the top and the bottom of the paper at the spiral, as shown.

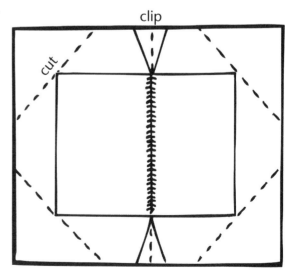

3 Again center the open notebook on the construction paper. Fold in the edges all the way around. Close the cover and run your thumb down the edges to crease them. Open and close the notebook several times to make sure it isn't too loose or too tight.

4 Open the notebook and spread glue along its edges, which will be covered by the construction paper. Press the construction paper in place and allow the glue to dry.

© 2007 by John Wiley & Sons, Inc.

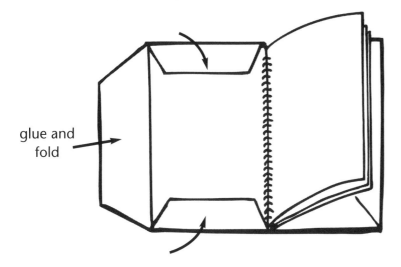

glue and fold

5 Write your name and a title on the cover using gold or silver ink. Your diary is now ready to record your thoughts.

In Their Own
WORDS

Could I have chosen my own genius and condition, I should have made myself a great poet.

ANDREW

JACKSON

Seventh President, 1829–1837

Born *March 15, 1767, Waxhaw Settlement, South Carolina*
Died *June 8, 1845, The Hermitage, Nashville, Tennessee*

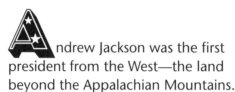 ndrew Jackson was the first president from the West—the land beyond the Appalachian Mountains. He was also the first to rise from humble beginnings, having been born in a log cabin in the rugged border region between North Carolina and South Carolina. He became one of the country's most popular presidents.

Jackson's experiences in the American Revolution left him with a strong sense of patriotism and a lifelong bitterness toward the British. As a fourteen-year-old militiaman, he was captured by British troops. When he refused to polish a British officer's boots, the officer struck him with his sword, leaving a permanent facial scar.

Although he had little formal education, Jackson studied law and moved to Tennessee, where he helped draft the state's constitution. He lived a rough-and-tumble frontier life but managed to become a successful plantation owner and judge.

Jackson became famous during the War of 1812. First, he defeated the Creek Indians at the Battle of Horseshoe Bend. Then in January 1815, he led a ragtag army against a British invasion force, winning a stirring victory in the Battle of New Orleans. Even though the battle was fought after a peace treaty had been signed, the victory gave Americans a great morale boost, and General Andrew Jackson was the nation's hero.

After a brief period in the U.S. Senate, Jackson ran for the presidency in 1824. Although he had the most votes in a four-man race, he did not have a majority of the electoral votes, and the House of Representatives awarded the election to John Quincy Adams. Jackson campaigned hard after this close race and won easily in 1828.

Jackson's popularity was aided by a wave of democratic feeling that was sweeping the country. Property qualifications for voting had been lowered or removed, so there were far more voters than ever before, including laborers who owned little or no

Family Matters

Jackson's wife, Rachel, died before he was inaugurated. The couple had no children of their own, but he adopted a nephew of Rachel's and named him Andrew Jackson Jr.

Nicknames

Jackson's opponents gave him nicknames like King Andrew, because of his strong rule. His supporters called him Old Hickory, a label created by his militia soldiers who said he was as "tough as old hickory."

20

property. Because of these changes, Jackson's two terms became known as Jacksonian Democracy. Jackson often said, "Let the people rule." But his belief in democracy was limited. He was a slave owner, for example, and he had no interest in ending slavery. And it was his presidency that produced the Indian Removal Act, forcing all Eastern tribes to move to "Indian Territory" beyond the Mississippi River.

After two terms as one of the nation's most popular presidents, Jackson retired to his Tennessee plantation, the Hermitage. He remained the country's elder statesman until his death in 1845. On his gravestone are these words: "His faith in the American people never wavered."

Blackberry Jam

President Jackson's favorite food was blackberry jam. You can use this nineteenth-century recipe with strawberries or raspberries, as well as blackberries.

1 Rinse the berries under cold running water and drain in a colander or large strainer.

2 Place the berries in a saucepan. Don't crush them.

3 Add 1 cup of sugar. With an adult's help, cook over low heat. Stir gently with a wooden spoon. Bring to the boiling point and boil for 3 minutes.

4 Gently stir in 1 cup of sugar. Bring to a boil again for 3 minutes.

5 Repeat with the third cup of sugar. Skim off any foam.

6 After the third 3-minute cooking, spoon the jam into a shallow bowl to cool. When the jam is cool, serve it on toast, or store it in covered jars in the refrigerator. It will keep for up to 2 weeks.

Things You'll Need

1 quart blackberries (or strawberries or raspberries)
3 cups sugar
adult helper
colander or strainer
2-quart saucepan
wooden spoon
shallow bowl
two 1-pint jars with lids
MAKES ABOUT 2 PINTS

Cherokee Bear Claw Necklace

Among the many Native American societies forced to move west by the Indian Removal Act, one of the largest was the Cherokee nation. The Cherokee were called one of the "five civilized tribes" because they had tried to adopt European ways of living, with settled farms, churches, and schools. More than one-third of the Cherokee died on the forced march called the Trail of Tears, from Georgia to what is now Oklahoma. You can make a Cherokee bear claw necklace to honor these courageous people.

1 Spread newspaper on your work surface. Open the package of clay and knead it for a few minutes to make it soft.

2 Pull off a small piece of clay. Flatten it with the heel of your hand, then work it into the bear claw shape, as shown in the drawing. Each "claw" should be about 1¼ inches long and ¼ inch thick. Use a craft stick or plastic picnic knife to create the curved shape. Use a knitting needle or nail to make a hole in the widest part of the claw.

3 Make 4 or 5 more claws.

Things You'll Need

several sheets of newspaper
package of self-hardening clay
ruler
craft stick or plastic picnic knife
knitting needle or large nail
acrylic paints—white, brown, and any other colors you choose
small paintbrush
rawhide lacing, about 22 inches (sold as shoelaces)

The Dueling President

According to legend, Jackson fought roughly a hundred duels. In one, his opponent shot first, hitting Jackson in the chest. Although staggered, Jackson shot and killed the other man. The bullet that injured Jackson was so close to his heart that doctors never tried to remove it.

4 Break off several smaller pieces of clay. Form them into 4 or 5 tube shapes to look like small bones, each about ¾ inch long. Carefully run the knitting needle or nail through each piece the long way to make a hole. (You might have to ask an adult to help you with this.)

5 Make about 10 small round beads from the clay, and make a hole through each.

6 Allow the pieces to dry according to the instructions on the package of clay.

7 Paint the claws brown. Paint the "bone" pieces white (unless the clay is already white). Paint the round bead pieces with the other colors you have chosen (red, blue, or yellow, for example).

8 When the paint is dry, string the clay pieces on the rawhide, alternating shapes, as shown. Tie the rawhide ends in a square knot or a tight double knot. Your Cherokee bear claw necklace is now ready to wear, or use it to decorate your room.

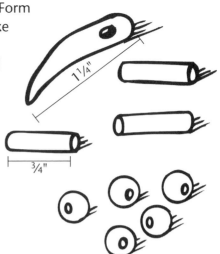

One man with courage makes a majority.

MARTIN VAN BUREN

Eighth President, 1837–1841

Born *December 5, 1782, Kinderhook, New York*
Died *July 24, 1862, Kinderhook, New York*

Following the dynamic personality of Andrew Jackson, Martin Van Buren seems to be one of the nation's less colorful presidents. He had many good qualities, however, including great skill as a politician. He was the dominant figure in New York State politics for more than thirty years, from 1820 to the mid-1850s. Unfortunately, his term as president was marred by economic factors he could not control. He himself summed up his time as president by saying, "As to the presidency, the two happiest days of my life were those of my entrance upon the office and my surrender of it."

Van Buren grew up in a small Hudson River town where his father was a farmer and tavern operator. After a few years of schooling, he began working in a lawyer's office at age fourteen and became a lawyer when he was twenty-one.

He was an ambitious young man and became a shrewd politician. He served in a number of New York State jobs, which he used to build up loyal political allies. He was elected to the U.S. Senate in 1821 and reelected six years later. Van Buren decided that his future success could be assured by allying himself with Andrew Jackson. He worked hard for Jackson's election in 1828, and Jackson rewarded him by naming him secretary of state. To become even closer to Jackson, Van Buren made it a point to ride with him every day even though he hated horseback riding. In 1832, he became Jackson's vice president, and four years later, he defeated William Henry Harrison for the presidency.

Almost as soon as Van Buren took the oath of office, the nation's economy crashed—one of the worst slumps in America's history. Thousands lost their jobs, and farm income fell sharply. The economic recession was not Van Buren's fault, but he had no idea how to help the country recover. And people were not pleased to see that the president continued to dress in expensive clothes and to enjoy imported wines with his meals. In the 1840 election, Van Buren lost to William Henry Harrison. Van Buren tried to make a comeback in 1844, but he lost the nomination to James K. Polk. He ran one more time, in 1848, and lost again. He retired to his home, Lindenwald, in Kinderhook, New York, where he died in 1862 at the age of eighty.

☆☆☆☆☆☆☆☆☆☆

Family Matters

Both Van Buren and his wife, Hannah, were of Dutch ancestry, and he often called her *Jannetje,* which is Dutch for "Hannah." She never lost her accent. After ten years of marriage, Hannah contracted tuberculosis and died in 1819. He never remarried. The Van Burens had four sons, all of whom played minor roles in politics.

☆☆☆☆☆☆☆☆☆☆

First Citizen

Van Buren was the first president born after American independence from Great Britain. That made him the first to be born an American citizen.

What's in a Name?

Unscramble the names and write them in the boxes. The shaded boxes will give you another scrambled word; unscramble it to find what all the others have in common.

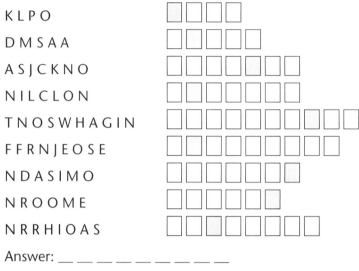

K L P O

D M S A A

A S J C K N O

N I L C L O N

T N O S W H A G I N

F F R N J E O S E

N D A S I M O

N R O O M E

N R R H I O A S

Answer: __ __ __ __ __ __ __ __

Answers appear at the back of the book.

Summer Wreath

Things You'll Need

adult helper
dried flowers
several sheets of newspaper
tub of water (or sink)
bundle of dry reeds (available at craft stores and many flower shops)
paper towels
twine
scissors
ribbon

When visitors approach Lindenwald, the Van Buren home in Kinderhook (now a historic site), they can expect to be greeted by an attractive, welcoming wreath on the door. This was a favorite nineteenth-century decoration in New York and New England at all times of the year, not just during Christmas. You can buy dried flowers or dry your own.

For dried flowers: With an adult's help, pick or buy fresh flowers and herbs, such as daisies, rosemary, marigolds, sage, and violets. Tie these in bunches with twine. Hang them upside down in a dark closet for 4 to 6 weeks. (You can also buy dried flowers at many craft stores.)

To make the wreath:

1 Spread newspaper on your work surface.

2 Fill a tub or sink with lukewarm water. Soak the reeds in it for 20 to 30 minutes to soften them. Dry them with paper towels.

3 Bend and mold the reeds into a circle, overlapping the ends. Tie them in several places with twine, as shown in the drawing.

Tie reeds to hold
them in place.

4 When the reeds are completely dry, add the dried flowers by pushing
   the stems in between the reeds. Use bits of twine or ribbon to hold
   them in place.

5 Use ribbon to tie a bow to the bottom of the wreath and
   hang your finished product on the door of your house or
   even on a wall of your room.

There is a power
in public opinion in this country—
and I thank God for it: for it is
the most honest and best
of all powers.

25

WILLIAM HENRY HARRISON

Ninth President, March–April 1841

Born *February 9, 1773, Charles City County, Virginia*
Died *April 4, 1841, Washington, D.C.*

William Henry Harrison had the unusual distinction of giving the longest Inaugural Address in history and having the shortest term in office. As you'll see, these two events are connected.

Although Harrison is not well known on the list of American presidents, he was a man of many talents. He was an outstanding scholar, for example. He entered Hampden-Sidney College when he was fourteen, studying Greek and Latin. He later studied medicine but then quit to go into the army.

Harrison became a tough and resourceful Indian fighter on the Northwest frontier, a sharpshooter who was also skilled with a tomahawk. At the age of twenty-seven, he was appointed governor of Indiana Territory, a post he held for twelve years. This was a huge territory, covering present-day Indiana, Illinois, Wisconsin, and large areas of Michigan and Minnesota. Indian uprisings were common here, as the region's Native Americans, numbering an estimated one hundred thousand, tried to hold back the advance of white settlers. It was Harrison's job to make the land safe for settlers, and he also hoped to treat the tribespeople with respect and dignity.

In the early 1800s, a great leader named Chief Tecumseh organized a large-scale force of several tribes. American forces, led by Harrison, fought the Native Americans to a draw at Tippecanoe, which later became Harrison's nickname. Then during the War of 1812, Harrison led American troops into Canada, where they beat the Native Americans and the British at the Battle of the Thames, and Tecumseh was killed, ending Native American resistance in the Northwest.

Harrison's presidential campaign against Van Buren in 1840 was lively and noisy. It was the first to feature colorful banners, torchlight parades, and many campaign songs. The slogan "Tippecanoe and Tyler, too" (referring to Vice President John Tyler), became one of the most popular in history.

Harrison won and took office in March 1841. Late in the month, he gave his Inaugural Address. On a cold, windy day, he spoke for nearly two hours. He caught a cold, which turned into pneumonia, and he died a few days later, exactly one month after taking office. He was the first president to die in office.

☆☆☆☆☆☆☆☆☆☆☆☆☆☆☆

Campaign Firsts

In the election campaign, Harrison was described as having been born in a log cabin to set him apart from Van Buren, who was seen as unsympathetic to the problems of the poor. Actually, Harrison had been born in a sixteen-room plantation house, but it started the campaign tradition of log-cabin origins.

One of Harrison's campaign banners was in the form of a large paper ball that was "rolled" from Kentucky to Baltimore, leading to the slogan, "Keep the ball rolling."

☆☆☆☆☆☆☆☆☆☆☆☆☆☆☆

Presidential Pet

The Harrisons had a pet goat named His Whiskers.

The Prophet's Curse?

When Chief Tecumseh was killed at the Battle of the Thames, his brother, known as the Prophet, placed a curse on Harrison "and all the leaders who follow him." Years later, people began to guess about this "curse." It was found that every president elected in a zero year (for example, 1840) died in office, and always in an odd-numbered year.

Use this book to test the so-called curse: Which presidents were elected in a year with a zero and died in an odd-numbered year? As you find each one, write the information in the appropriate spaces. The first one is done for you. Be sure to include data for the one president who ended the curse by being elected in a zero year but not dying in an odd-numbered year. Find out who finally broke the string of coincidence.

President's Name	Year Elected	Year Died
1 William Henry Harrison	1840	1841
2		
3		
4		
5		
6		

President Who Broke the "Curse"	Year Elected	Year Died

Answers appear at the back of the book.

Campaign Banner

To celebrate the first modern-style election campaign in 1840, make your own campaign banner. The subject can be your own favorite political candidate, or choose a theme not connected to an election, such as an environmental issue or a favorite sports team.

1 Spread newspaper over your work surface. Cut the pillowcase, bedsheet, or butcher paper to fit the width of the coat hanger. Make the banner as long as you want.

2 On a piece of scrap paper, plan the words and pictures you want. You can also draw rough outlines on the cloth or butcher paper.

3 Carefully paint symbols and letters on the banner. Rinse your brush as needed in the cup of water.

4 When the paint is dry, fold the top of the banner over the hanger. Use needle and thread to sew the banner in place, or you can staple it instead. Hang the banner in your room.

Family Matters

Anna Tuthill Symmes, who married Harrison in 1795, became the only first lady never to live in the official presidential residence. She had not yet left their home in North Bend, Ohio, when Harrison died.

The Harrisons had 10 children—6 sons and 4 daughters. These offspring provided 48 grandchildren, the most of any president, and 106 great-grandchildren, also a record. One grandson, Benjamin Harrison, became the twenty-third president.

Things You'll Need

several sheets of newspaper
old white pillowcase, bedsheet, or a long piece of white butcher paper
scissors
coat hanger (wood, if possible)
pencil and scrap paper
tempera paints
paintbrushes
paper cup of water
needle and thread, or a stapler

In Their Own

The people are the best guardians of their own rights, and it is the duty of their executive to abstain from interfering.

27

John Tyler

Tenth President, 1841–1845

Born *March 29, 1790, Charles City County, Virginia*
Died *January 18, 1862, Richmond, Virginia*

hen William Henry Harrison died after only a month in office, no one knew what to expect when Vice President John Tyler succeeded him. All of the eight earlier presidents had served their full terms. Many thought that Tyler would become a kind of caretaker president, allowing Congress and the cabinet to make important decisions. John Tyler, however, had no intention of being a figurehead.

Tyler had always been an ambitious person and brilliant as well. He was born into a wealthy Virginia family; his father was governor of Virginia and a close friend of Thomas Jefferson. Tyler graduated from William and Mary College at age seventeen and was a lawyer within two years. A tall, courteous man, he made friends easily and rose quickly through the political ranks. He served in the House of Representatives, as the governor of Virginia, and then as a U.S. senator.

In 1840, he was chosen as the Whig Party's candidate for vice president. Party leaders had chosen a military hero, Harrison, to head the ticket, and Tyler's popularity in the South provided a good balance. Tyler, however, refused to cooperate when told that Harrison had agreed that the cabinet would make all important decisions. He made it clear that he intended to be president in his own right, and he twice vetoed one of the Whig Party's favorite projects.

Furious at Tyler's independence, the Whig leaders voted him out of the party, and every member of the cabinet resigned. Tyler named a new cabinet, but he was now a president without a party. Newspapers referred to him as His Accidency, and Tyler wrote that he was forced to serve in an office that was a "bed of thorns."

Tyler completed his term in the same independent spirit with which he had started. His last act as president, three days before leaving office, was to sign a measure annexing Texas. He then retired to his Virginia home, where he and his second wife, Julia Gardner Tyler, started what was for him a second family. His final political act involved trying to arrange a compromise between the North and the South on the eve of the Civil War. He died in 1862.

His determination to be a president in his own right established an important precedent. Since Tyler, every vice president who succeeded to the office has followed his model.

Tyler Firsts

In addition to being the first vice president to succeed to the presidency, John Tyler was also the first to have no vice president during his entire term, to have a wife die while he was in office, to marry while in office, and to have a wife who was younger than some of her stepchildren.

Family Matters

After a happy marriage of twenty-nine years with his first wife, Letitia, who died in 1842, Tyler shocked people by remarrying two years later. The president was fifty-four years old and his bride was a twenty-four-year-old beauty, Julia Gardner, known as the Rose of Long Island. The lively new first lady quickly won over Washington society. She also adapted the words of the song "Hail to the Chief" for her husband, and it has remained the official song of the president.

After having eight children with his first wife, Tyler had seven more with his second. The last was born in 1860, when Tyler was seventy. He died two years later.

Word Search

The following sentence contains ten underlined words and names associated with John Tyler's life and presidency. All ten are hidden in the puzzle. As you find each word or name, draw a line around it. The hidden words can read left to right, right to left, up, down, or on a diagonal.

John <u>Tyler</u> of <u>Virginia</u>, defying former <u>Whig</u> <u>cabinet</u> members, signed a measure annexing <u>Texas</u>, then ended his <u>term</u> as <u>president</u>, retiring with his <u>first</u> <u>lady</u> and all their <u>children</u>.

Answers appear at the back of the book.

```
L C A R Y E R X T B L R
R V B V I R G I N I A G
E Y N S G M A Y M N W I
W R H T N E D I S E R P
G I F E W A Y L P R N G
T S O X L D R E N D H C
P D M A B R A T Y L E R
F I R S T N W O W I R L
H E R Y P E T I J H K P
V I M C L H R F N C I R
T E N I B A C M N M S G
```

The Game of Marbles

John Tyler loved children, and parties for the family's children were almost daily happenings in the White House and the Tylers' Virginia home. He also loved playing games with his children. According to legend, he was playing marbles with two of his sons on the living room floor of the Virginia house when word came that Harrison had died and he was now president of the United States.

There are many different marble games that have been popular since the 1800s. Although most versions are played outdoors, a simple game called Straight Shot can be played indoors. A bare floor or linoleum are better than a carpet for marble games.

The official way to shoot a marble requires keeping the knuckles of your index and middle fingers on the ground. Hold the marble in the crook of your index finger and flick the marble with your thumb.

Rules for Straight Shot:

1 Each player places 3 marbles in a line.

2 Shooting from the same spot (somewhere between 3 and 7 feet from the line), the players take turns shooting. Players keep any marbles they knock off the line, setting these winners aside.

3 If a player misses—hits no marbles—she adds another of her marbles to the line.

4 The game continues until all marbles have been knocked off the line. The player with the most marbles wins.

I can never consent to being dictated to.

29

James Knox Polk

Eleventh President, 1845–1849

Born November 2, 1795, Mecklenberg, North Carolina
Died June 15, 1849, Nashville, Tennessee

James Knox Polk became president at a time when Americans were convinced of their Manifest Destiny—the idea that it was the clear (or manifest) destiny of the United States to have boundaries that stretched from the Atlantic Ocean to the Pacific. As president, Polk was determined to make Manifest Destiny a reality by bringing Texas, California, and Oregon into the Union.

Born in North Carolina, Polk was barely ten when his family moved west to Tennessee, a 500-mile journey by covered wagon. He was too sickly to be of much help on his family's frontier farm, so he concentrated on his education. After graduating with honors from the University of North Carolina, he studied law and decided on a career in politics.

Polk proved to be a good political organizer and rapidly rose to the top of the Democratic Party in Tennessee. After serving in the state legislature, he was elected to the House of Representatives, where he served seven terms (1825–1839), the last four years as Speaker of the House. He was a loyal supporter of Andrew Jackson and worked hard to promote Old Hickory's program in Congress. In 1839, he retired from Congress to pursue the governorship of Tennessee, but he was defeated in 1841 and again in 1843.

In 1844, he was hoping to be nominated for the vice presidency. But when Van Buren repeatedly failed to get the two-thirds vote needed for the presidential nomination, Andrew Jackson advanced Polk's name. Polk won the presidential nomination and went on to defeat Henry Clay in the election.

Polk's predecessor, John Tyler, had annexed Texas, but Polk wanted Texas to be in the Union. So he used a dispute over the Texas-Mexico boundary to maneuver Mexico into war in 1846. After a long and difficult struggle, the Americans won, and in 1848 all of Mexico's lands in the West, including California, New Mexico, Arizona, Nevada, and parts of Utah and Colorado, became part of the United States.

Polk's other great achievement was settling a dispute with Great Britain over the territory of Oregon, which extended along the Pacific Coast from Alaska to California. While many were ready to go to war for Oregon if necessary, Polk managed a peaceful settlement. With the addition of this territory, Polk now presided over a nation that extended from coast to coast, and Manifest Destiny was a reality. During his presidency, the country had grown by roughly 800,000 square miles.

☆☆☆☆☆☆☆☆☆☆

Family Matters

Polk and his wife, Sarah Childress Polk, had a long and happy marriage. As first lady, she banned dancing and hard liquor from White House functions. She hosted the first Thanksgiving dinner at the White House, which has been an annual affair ever since. She and James had no children. After Polk's death in 1849, she remained in their Nashville home until her death in 1891, at the age of eighty-seven.

☆☆☆☆☆☆☆☆☆☆

Wired News

News of Polk's presidential nomination was the first to be spread by telegraph. People were so surprised by Jackson's choice that they wondered if something was wrong with the telegraph.

Few presidents worked as hard as Polk, even though he was never physically strong. Worn out and sick, he died barely three months after leaving office.

The Magic of Morse Code

Although Samuel F. B. Morse had patented the telegraph in 1837, it was not until 1844 that the government allocated the money to develop this revolutionary form of communication. After the telegraph system was set up, messages that had taken days or even weeks to deliver were now completed in a matter of minutes. Messages were sent through wires by tapping on keys, but you'll find it easier to distinguish dots and dashes by using flashlight signals.

Things You'll Need

partner
2 pencils
2 pieces of paper
2 flashlights

1 Practice by writing out a word or two using dots and dashes for letters, as shown in the chart. You'll quickly see the advantage of keeping messages short and simple.

2 Write out a short message to your partner in Morse code, while he or she writes one to you. Leave a space between letters. For example:

  · · · ·   ·   · — · ·   · — · ·   — — —
    H   E   L   L   O

3 Take turns using the flashlights to exchange the messages. Use long and short flashes to convey dashes and dots. As you receive your partner's message, jot down the dots and dashes on paper, then decipher them.

MORSE CODE		
A · —	N — ·	1 · — — — —
B — · · ·	O — — —	2 · · — — —
C — · — ·	P · — — ·	3 · · · — —
D — · ·	Q — — · —	4 · · · · —
E ·	R · — ·	5 · · · · ·
F · · — ·	S · · ·	6 — · · · ·
G — — ·	T —	7 — — · · ·
H · · · ·	U · · —	8 — — — · ·
I · ·	V · · · —	9 — — — — ·
J · — — —	W · — —	0 — — — — —
K — · —	X — · · —	
L · — · ·	Y — · — —	
M — —	Z — — · ·	

Beginning of transmission — · — · —
Error · · · · · · · ·
End of transmission · — · — ·
period · — · — · —
comma — — · · — —
question · · — — · ·

A Risky Operation

One reason Polk was sickly as a boy was that he suffered from gallstones. The pain became so great that at age sixteen, he went to a frontier surgeon who dared to perform gallbladder surgery in the days before anesthesia and sterilized instruments. Young Polk survived and his health improved.

Capirotada, or Spotted Dog

Things You'll Need

1 cup raisins

1 cup hot water

4 eggs

2 cups milk

1 cup light brown sugar

1½ cups peeled and sliced apples

1½ teaspoons cinnamon

1 teaspoon nutmeg

3 slices of white bread, dry or lightly toasted

4 ounces unsalted butter, melted

1 cup grated cheddar cheese

adult helper

measuring cup

measuring spoon

small bowl

large bowl

egg beater

wooden spoon

2-quart casserole dish

oven mitts

Makes 4–5 servings

When the United States won the Mexican War, Mexico gave up California and all the lands of what is now the American Southwest. Thousands of people of Hispanic background suddenly found themselves living in American territory. These new Americans added a great deal to the nation's culture, including crafts, architecture, music, foods, and words. Here is a great dessert introduced to the lands north of the Rio Grande. The Mexican people called it Spotted Dog. You won't have any trouble figuring out how it got that name.

1 Have an adult preheat the oven to 350 degrees F.

2 Place the raisins in a small bowl and pour a cup of hot water over them. Let them soak a minute or two, then drain.

3 Break the eggs into a large bowl. Beat them well. Add the milk and stir thoroughly. Add the brown sugar and stir.

4 Stir in the apples, cinnamon, and nutmeg.

5 Break the bread into small pieces and add them to the mixture. Stir in the melted butter. Add the raisins and mix thoroughly.

6 Pour half the mixture into a 2-quart casserole. Sprinkle ½ cup of the cheese over the top.

7 Pour the rest of the mixture into the casserole and top it with the rest of the cheese.

8 Bake at 350 degrees F for 45 minutes. Have an adult use oven mitts to remove the casserole from the oven. Let it cool for 10 to 15 minutes. Serve warm.

In Their Own Words

No president who performs his duties faithfully and conscientiously can have any leisure.

ZACHARY TAYLOR

Twelfth President, 1849–1850

Born *November 24, 1784, Orange County, Virginia*
Died *July 9, 1850, Washington, D.C.*

Like Andrew Jackson twenty years earlier, Zachary Taylor was a great military hero. He took office at a time when the issue of slavery threatened to destroy the Union. Since Taylor was a Southerner and the owner of more than a hundred slaves, those who supported slavery in the new lands of the West felt he was the perfect choice to be chief executive. But the pro-slave forces failed to consider Taylor's commitment to the Union.

Although born in Virginia, Taylor grew up on the Western frontier near Louisville, Kentucky. He had very little schooling and then settled on a career in the army, serving almost forty years, from 1808 to 1848. Taylor slowly rose through the army's ranks while fighting in the War of 1812, the Black Hawk War (1832), the Second Seminole War in Florida (1837–1840), and the Mexican War (1846–1848).

In 1846, President Polk sent General Taylor to the disputed border area between Texas and Mexico. The move provoked Mexico into war. Taylor won impressive victories in 1846, but after Taylor gave his enemy generous terms at his victory at Monterey, an angered Polk took away most of his troops. Instead of resigning, Taylor continued to fight. Again Taylor won a stirring victory, this time against the great Mexican general Santa Anna, and news of the triumph made him a national hero.

Taylor was encouraged to run for the presidency and won the election. As he took office, California was seeking admission to the Union as a free state (a state in which slavery was not allowed). This would have upset the balance between free states and slave states in the Union (there were fifteen of each at that time).

Southern leaders vowed to leave the Union unless the balance of states was preserved, and they counted on Taylor's support. Instead, the new president said he intended to do all in his power to preserve the Union, threatening to personally lead an army against any state that tried to leave.

A Fitting Name

Taylor's men called him Old Rough and Ready, an affectionate nickname that originated in part from his habit of wearing whatever clothes he had at hand, often mixing farm clothes with worn-out bits of uniform.

Family Matters

Taylor's wife, Margaret "Peggy" Smith Taylor, dutifully followed her husband from one military base to the next while also giving birth to four children. She was so eager to stay at their Louisiana home that she prayed he would lose the 1848 election. She was ill much of her time as first lady and left official duties to one of her daughters, Mrs. Elizabeth Bliss.

Another daughter, Sarah, married one of her father's officers—Jefferson Davis—who became president of the Confederacy in 1861.

Before the issue was settled, Taylor became ill at a ceremony at the Washington Monument on July 4, 1850. He may have suffered a heart attack or he may have been made ill by consuming huge quantities of cherries. In any case, President Taylor died four days later, after only sixteen months in office.

Poke Pouch

© 2007 by John Wiley & Sons, Inc.

When General Taylor was sent to the Texas-Mexico border, he discovered the world of Mexican *vaqueros*, the cowboys who herded the long-horned cattle roaming the region. Taylor and his men were fascinated by the cowboys' equipment, including a simple shawl called a *serape* and broad-brimmed hats that protected against sun and rain. Here are directions for another favorite item: the poke pouch. American cowboys used it to store their "poke," such as pipes, tobacco, matches, and a little money.

1 On one piece of fabric, turn down the top edge about ½ inch. Sew close to the edge, leaving a tube, or casing, which will hold the drawstring.

2 Repeat with the other piece of fabric.

3 Use straight pins to pin the two fabric pieces together, with the casing facing out. Sew along the side edge, across the bottom, and up the other side. Start and end the sewing *below* the casing. (In other words, don't sew the casing closed.)

4 Turn the pouch right side out.

5 Fasten a safety pin to one end of a rawhide lace or ribbon. Use the safety pin to push the rawhide lace through the casing. Repeat with the other lace through the other casing, as shown.

6 Knot the ends of the cords on one side so that they don't slide out of the casing. Tie the cords on the other side in a bow or square knot so that you can open and close the pouch.

Things You'll Need

2 pieces of chamois or brown felt, about 6 × 8 inches (chamois is available in automotive departments)

scissors

ruler

needle and thread (or use a sewing machine with an adult's help)

straight pins

safety pin

two 11-inch pieces of rawhide lacing (sold as shoelaces, or substitute a narrow piece of ribbon if you prefer)

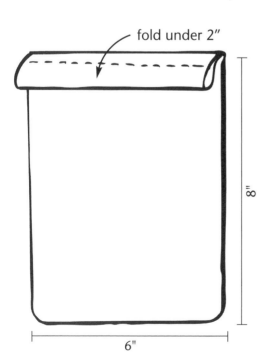

fold under 2"

8"

6"

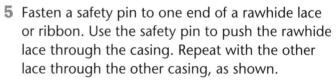

Alphabet Scramble

Each of the empty boxes needs one letter of the alphabet to form a word or name of three letters or more from Zachary Taylor's life. The letter you insert can be at the beginning, at the end, or in the middle of the word. The letters will come from the last fifteen letters of the alphabet—L to Z.

Each letter will be used only once, so cross off each one as you use it. All the words read across, from left to right. In the first row across, we've used the Q to form VAQUEROS.

© 2007 by John Wiley & Sons, Inc.

L M N O P Q̸ R S T U V W X Y Z

```
X L V A [Q] U E R O S D F
M O R B [ ] A C K H A W K
D Q P F [ ] I C T O R Y E
B R N P [ ] L K A C W I N
D A M J [ ] O U G H P S R
O G R U [ ] I F O R M B W
A M S T [ ] O L D I E R A
X O M E [ ] I C O F N W Y
L B T A [ ] L O R D P S G
N D C O [ ] A R G A R E T
S E R A [ ] E R T Y Z G P
W A B L [ ] N I O N X W A
M R G O [ ] A C H A R Y M
A S A N [ ] A A N N A L O
I B O L [ ] A R P W D E X
```

Answers appear at the back of the book.

An Empty Resumé

Zachary Taylor was the first president to have had no previous political experience. In fact, he never voted in any election, not even his own.

Return to Sender

When Taylor won the 1848 nomination, Whig leaders sent a letter to his Louisiana plantation to inform him. As was common practice, there was no postage on the letter; Taylor had to pay the postage to receive it. Since he was being swamped by similar letters from well-wishers, Taylor refused to pay the postage. Weeks passed before party leaders figured out what had happened and finally sent a prepaid notice.

Whatever dangers may threaten [the Union], I shall stand by it and maintain it . . . to the full extent . . . of the power conferred upon me by the Constitution.

MILLARD FILLMORE

Thirteenth President, 1850–1853

Born *January 7, 1800, Cayuga County, New York*
Died *March 8, 1874, Buffalo, New York*

illard Fillmore was one of the few presidents to rise from truly humble origins. He was born in a log cabin in what was then the wilderness of New York State's Finger Lakes region. Throughout his career, he was staunchly anti-slavery, but he also believed that the North and South could reach a compromise that would avoid war.

Working on the family farm, he became a strong, husky youth, but he longed to see the larger world. His father indentured him to a cloth maker, but the boy hated the work and managed to buy back his contract. Although he had little formal schooling, Fillmore discovered the world of books and became an avid reader. When he was nineteen, he enrolled in a new school, where he became a favorite of the teacher, Abigail Powers. They married a few years later.

Fillmore moved to Buffalo, where he taught school and studied law. After being admitted to the bar, he established a law practice and entered politics. He was elected to Congress in 1832, serving in the House of Representatives until 1843. In 1844, he narrowly lost the election for governor of New York. Four years later, he became Zachary Taylor's vice president.

When Taylor died in July 1850, Fillmore became the president. At the time, Congress had worked out what was called the Compromise of 1850: in exchange for California's admission to the Union, Congress would pass the Fugitive Slave Law. This allowed agents for slave owners to capture escaped slaves anywhere, including the free states of the North. Taylor had planned to veto the compromise, but Fillmore felt it was the nation's best hope for unity and approved it. This action cost him the support of many Northerners.

Fillmore was not eager to run for election in 1852. In a letter to the Whig Party convention, he asked the party "not to suffer my name to be dragged into a contest for a nomination which I have never sought and do not now seek." He did not win the nomination.

Family Matters

First Lady Abigail Fillmore, with her husband's help, persuaded Congress to provide funds for the first White House library. During the Fillmores' three years there, the White House kitchen also received a stove (cooking had previously been done in a large fireplace) and running water was installed.

Abigail Fillmore became ill during Fillmore's term in the White House. She left many of the official duties to her daughter, Mary Abigail Fillmore, a skilled musician who often entertained guests on the piano, harp, or guitar.

Abigail Fillmore died of pneumonia in 1853. In 1858, Millard Fillmore married a wealthy widow named Caroline Carmichael McIntosh.

In 1856, the America Party, also known as the Know-Nothings, nominated Fillmore for president. He finished third behind James Buchanan and John C. Fremont, the first candidate of the new Republican Party. Fillmore retired from politics and lived with his second wife, Caroline, until his death in 1874.

Pressed Flower Bookmark

After Commodore Perry's visit to Japan in 1853, Japanese products, including a variety of crafts, began to appear in American shops and stores. One kind of craft that appealed to Americans was called *ikebana*—the arrangement of plant materials to illustrate an idea, such as peacefulness, or the seasons.

In this project, you can use plant materials to make a colorful bookmark. You may want to make several to give as gifts.

For pressed flowers: Pick blossoms, ferns, and leaves when they are dry. Choose blossoms that aren't thick. Pansies are ideal because they're flat and colorful.

Place the plant material between sheets of clean paper. Don't overlap them. Place the sheets between the pages of a large book and stack other books on top. Allow the plants to dry in this press for about 2 weeks.

To make the bookmark:

1 Spread newspaper on your work surface. Place your plant materials on top of the newspaper.

2 Cut a piece of heavyweight construction paper about 8 inches long and 2½ inches wide. Arrange some of the plant materials on the construction paper. Try not to handle the plants too much. When you have an arrangement you like, glue the pieces to the construction paper. A touch of glue on each piece is enough.

3 Cut a piece of plastic wrap or contact paper larger than your bookmark. Fit it over the bookmark. Cut off the corners as shown in the drawing. Then fold the plastic onto the back and glue it down, or skip the glue if you're using contact paper. (If the back looks too messy, glue a piece of thin construction paper over it.)

4 For an added touch, punch a hole in a top corner of your bookmark and loosely tie a piece of yarn or ribbon to it.

Things You'll Need

fresh flower blossoms, leaves, ferns
several sheets of clean paper
stacks of books
several sheets of newspaper
scissors
sheet of heavyweight construction paper in a pastel color
white glue
clear plastic wrap or contact paper
sheet of lightweight construction paper
hole punch
scrap of yarn or ribbon

cut away corner

8"

2½"

37

Alphabet Scramble

This Alphabet Scramble follows the same rules as the Zachary Taylor one on page 35, but this time you'll use only the first part of the alphabet, from A to K.

A B C D E F G H I J K

Remember to cross off each letter as you use it. All the words read across, from left to right.

A	L	M	C	☐	Y	U	G	A	R	W	B
R	F	U	B	☐	L	E	C	T	S	M	X
M	W	M	A	☐	I	G	A	I	L	D	R
S	E	B	L	☐	A	P	A	N	O	N	F
T	W	H	I	☐	L	D	W	N	M	R	Y
R	M	B	U	☐	F	A	L	O	S	E	A
T	N	R	F	☐	O	U	S	E	Y	B	L
N	A	S	B	☐	N	O	W	L	D	E	M
N	O	T	H	☐	N	G	B	R	A	W	L
L	M	I	N	☐	E	N	T	U	R	E	D
Y	B	F	M	☐	A	R	O	L	I	N	E

Answers appear at the back of the book.

☆☆☆☆☆☆☆☆☆☆☆☆☆☆☆☆☆☆☆☆☆☆☆☆

Opening Japan

One of the most lasting achievements of Millard Fillmore's presidency occurred in 1853 when he sent Commodore Matthew Perry on a diplomatic voyage to Japan. Perry persuaded the Japanese government to allow trade with American merchants. This "opening" of Japan represented the first time that it had allowed any trade with Western countries since the 1600s.

☆☆☆☆☆☆☆☆☆☆☆☆☆☆☆☆☆☆☆☆☆☆☆☆

In Their Own WORDS

It is a national disgrace that our presidents ... should be cast adrift and perhaps be compelled to keep a corner grocery for subsistence.

38

FRANKLIN PIERCE

Fourteenth President, 1853–1857

Born November 23, 1804, Hillsboro, New Hampshire
Died October 8, 1869, Concord, New Hampshire

Franklin Pierce had many of the qualities needed to become a popular and successful president. A tall, handsome man who made friends easily, he was also a brilliant trial lawyer and had served as a brigadier general in the Mexican War (1846–1848). But everything he did in his four years as president seemed to reduce his popularity.

Pierce was born into a leading New Hampshire family. After graduating from Bowdoin College, he became a lawyer and a politician. After serving in the state legislature and in both houses of Congress, he volunteered in the Mexican War, serving under General Winfield Scott, who became his opponent in the election of 1852.

When the Democratic convention met to choose a candidate, Pierce's name was not even mentioned until the convention became hopelessly deadlocked, having voted forty times without selecting a candidate. Pierce's name was then offered as a dark horse, or compromise, candidate. He won the nomination and then beat Scott in the election.

As president, Pierce argued that slavery was protected by the Constitution and that Congress should not interfere with it. This disturbed antislavery forces in the North, and his popularity dropped. And when violence erupted in Kansas Territory over the slavery issue, Pierce's failure to stop the bloodshed damaged his reputation further.

He ran into more trouble when he began searching for ways to add to U.S. territory. In 1854, a newspaper published a government memo known as the Ostend Manifesto. The document revealed that Pierce's administration was illegally trying to take Cuba from Spain. People throughout the North were furious. They saw it as an effort to add land that would be another slave state.

When the Democratic Party met to choose a candidate for 1856, they did not consider offering Pierce a chance for reelection. He retired to New Hampshire, where he watched helplessly as the nation drifted into the Civil War (1861–1865). When he spoke out against the war, angry mobs threatened to burn his home. By the time of his death in 1869, Pierce had few friends even in his home state.

☆☆☆☆☆☆☆☆☆☆

College Pals

Pierce attended Bowdoin College in Maine, a small school at the time, with fewer than twenty in each graduating class. Two of his friends, both a year behind him, became leading figures in American literature: Henry Wadsworth Longfellow and Nathaniel Hawthorne.

☆☆☆☆☆☆☆☆☆☆

Family Matters

Tragedy struck the Pierces shortly before his inauguration when their only living son, Benjamin (Bennie), was killed in a train accident. (Their other two sons had died several years earlier.) First Lady Jane Pierce never got over the loss. For two years, dressed in black, she remained "the shadow in the White House," leaving formal functions to her aunt and to Varina Davis, wife of the secretary of war. She finally took up some of her duties but remained a "frail and melancholy figure."

The Map Maker's Challenge

The United States was growing rapidly. As new states were added, map makers drew new boundaries. They also followed a color rule to make their maps easy to read: regions that touched must be colored differently. At first, they used many colors. Then it was discovered that only four colors were needed on any map to be sure that no areas that touched were the same color, even in a map of the United States.

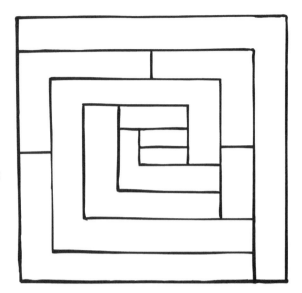

1 The following diagram is not a map, but it presents the same challenge. Using just 4 colors, see if you can color all the regions so that regions of the same color do not touch. *Hint:* Before you start filling in regions, pencil in the name of the color to work out the pattern.

2 Using the same color rule, color in the map of the eastern United States.

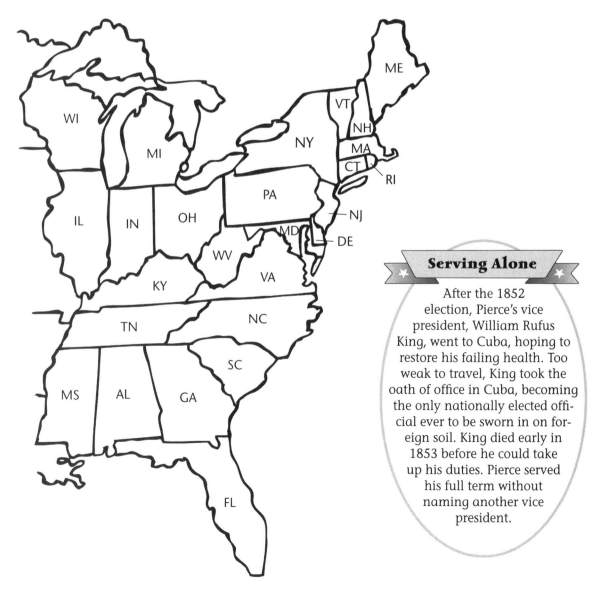

★ Serving Alone ★

After the 1852 election, Pierce's vice president, William Rufus King, went to Cuba, hoping to restore his failing health. Too weak to travel, King took the oath of office in Cuba, becoming the only nationally elected official ever to be sworn in on foreign soil. King died early in 1853 before he could take up his duties. Pierce served his full term without naming another vice president.

Maple Spice Cake

As a New Hampshire native, Franklin Pierce would have been familiar with this tasty recipe. It was a Concord, New Hampshire, specialty beginning in the early 1800s.

1 Have an adult preheat the oven to 350 degrees F.

2 Grease a 9-inch square baking pan with butter.

3 Sift the flour, baking powder, salt, cinnamon, ginger, and nutmeg into a large bowl. Set this aside.

4 Break 2 eggs into a second large bowl and beat them. In another bowl, use an egg beater or mixer to cream the butter until light and fluffy. Add the butter, maple syrup, applesauce, and milk to the eggs.

5 Gradually add the dry ingredients to the liquid mixture, stirring constantly. Blend thoroughly with the egg beater or mixer.

6 Pour the batter into the baking pan. Bake at 350 degrees F for 45 to 50 minutes. Have an adult use oven mitts to remove the pan from the oven. Cool for 30 minutes and frost with white frosting.

Things You'll Need

1½ cups all-purpose flour
2 teaspoons baking powder
½ teaspoon salt
½ teaspoon cinnamon
⅛ teaspoon ginger
¼ teaspoon nutmeg
2 eggs
4 ounces unsalted butter at room temperature
1 cup maple syrup
1 cup applesauce
⅓ cup milk
1 pint white frosting
adult helper
measuring cup
measuring spoon
9-inch square baking pan
sifter
3 large bowls
egg beater or mixer
wooden spoon
oven mitts
table knife
MAKES 8–10 SERVINGS

How futile are all our efforts to maintain the Union by force of arms.

James Buchanan

Fifteenth President, 1857–1861

Born *April 23, 1791, Cove Gap, Pennsylvania*
Died *June 1, 1868, Wheatland Estate, Lancaster, Pennsylvania*

For much of his life, James Buchanan wanted to be president. And he looked the part: tall and broad-shouldered, with wavy gray hair and piercing blue eyes. After several near-misses, he finally won the presidency in 1856, only to suffer through four unhappy years. He wrote to his successor, Abraham Lincoln: "My dear sir, if you are as happy on entering the White House as I on leaving, you are a very happy man indeed."

Buchanan grew up in rural Pennsylvania. After graduating from Dickinson College in 1809, he studied law, built a remarkably successful law practice, and entered politics. Following a term in the state legislature, he suffered a devastating personal loss when his fiancée, Ann Coleman, died suddenly in 1819. Buchanan vowed never to marry and later became the only president never to marry.

In 1820, he was elected to the House of Representatives, winning five two-year terms. Later he served as U.S. minister to Russia, then won two terms in the Senate in 1834 and 1840. By this time, Buchanan was longing to be president. He tried for the Democratic nomination in 1848 but lost, then lost again in 1852. When President Pierce made him minister to England in 1853, his dreams of the presidency seemed to be over. But two months after his return, he won the 1856 nomination and then the election.

Buchanan's presidency seemed doomed from the start as the conflict over the slavery issue grew steadily worse. He was dedicated to preserving the Union and he hated slavery. But he also felt he was helpless to act. For years he had insisted that "slavery is an evil without a remedy." The hardest time for Buchanan was the period between Lincoln's election in November 1860 and his being sworn in as president in March 1861. Buchanan was still president during those four months, as one Southern state after another withdrew, or seceded, from the Union. As with slavery, he felt he had no authority to act, so he did nothing.

Buchanan was relieved to go into retirement, even though the press and some members of Congress blamed him for his failure to act. He remained at his Wheatland estate in Pennsylvania, surrounded by more than twenty nieces and nephews, until his death in 1868.

Family Matters

Since Buchanan was not married, one of his nieces, Harriet Lane, served as hostess at the White House functions. In her mid-twenties and well educated, she enjoyed great popularity.

The song "Listen to the Mockingbird" was written in her honor. And the first shots fired by a Union ship in the Civil War came from a Coast Guard cutter named the *Harriet Lane*.

Confused States

As the slavery issue tore the nation apart, there was confusion over which states were trying to leave the Union and which would remain loyal. The border areas between North and South were particularly uncertain.

In tribute to those "states of confusion," see if you can identify the twelve states outlined here. *Note:* The position of the states and relation to each other is not accurate. We've also altered the relative size to add to the confusion. So the only thing you have to go by are the shapes.

Answers appear at the back of the book.

College Days

At Dickinson College, Buchanan got in trouble with authorities and was asked to leave. He promised to mend his ways and was allowed to stay. No details of his rowdy behavior were ever made public.

© 2007 by John Wiley & Sons, Inc.

☆☆☆☆☆☆☆☆☆☆☆

Royal Exchanges

Buchanan had established a friendship with the English royal family during his years in London as U.S. minister. In 1858, Buchanan exchanged transatlantic telegrams with Queen Victoria, becoming the first president to use the transatlantic cable.

In 1860, Prince Albert Edward, who became King Edward VII, visited the United States and was a guest at the White House. The prince slept in Buchanan's bed, while the president made do on a couch in the hall.

☆☆☆☆☆☆☆☆☆☆☆

Decoupage

Scrapbooks were a popular pastime in the mid-1800s. People pasted pictures from magazines, advertisements, and postage stamps in their scrapbooks. Companies even published sheets of pictures called "scraps" to cut up for collections. One of Buchanan's nieces, Harriet Lane, collected a variety of mementos from her three years in London when her uncle was U.S. minister and put them in scrapbooks.

Another popular use of scraps was for decoupage—covering a box or other object with pictures. Here are easy directions for making a decoupage box.

1 Spread newspaper on your work surface. Cut the magazine pictures into different shapes.

2 Experiment with different arrangements on the lid and sides of your box. When you have an arrangement you like, glue the pieces in place, leaving as little of the box showing as possible. Cover the entire back of each picture with glue so that no corners turn up.

3 When the glue has dried, use a paintbrush to cover the entire surface with 2 coats of acrylic varnish. Allow 1 hour drying time between coats. (*Note:* Acrylic varnish is not oil-based, so it is safe to use.)

In Their Own WORDS

I believe [slavery] to be a great political and a great moral evil. I thank God, my lot has been cast in a State where it does not exist.

Abraham Lincoln

Sixteenth President, 1861–1865

Born *February 12, 1809, Hardin County, Kentucky*
Died *April 15, 1865, Washington, D.C.*

For much of his career, including the presidency, Abraham Lincoln was severely criticized by the press and by political leaders. But common people, like farmers, shopkeepers, and city workers, had great confidence in him. Like many of the people who supported him, Lincoln had risen from humble beginnings and had to overcome many obstacles. He also had a remarkable genius for explaining complex issues in ways that people could understand. These qualities helped him interpret difficult concepts, such as the debate over slavery and the Civil War, and made him one of our greatest presidents.

Lincoln was born in a log cabin on the Kentucky frontier. His father, Thomas, was a struggling farmer who moved the family often in his search for success. Young Abraham had only about a year of formal schooling but managed to educate himself by reading every book he could borrow. He also worked a variety of jobs and twice failed in running a store. He studied law, opened a practice, and was elected to the Illinois legislature, where he served from 1834 to 1846.

In 1846, Lincoln won a seat in the House of Representatives, but he opposed the war with Mexico and was not reelected. He disappeared from public life for a few years, returning when the Republican Party was formed. He was dedicated to preventing the expansion of slavery into the new lands of the West. He lost a bid for the Senate seat held by Democrat Stephen A. Douglas, but his seven debates with the famous Douglas made Lincoln a national figure. The Republicans nominated Lincoln for the presidency in 1860, and he had a narrow victory.

By the spring of 1861, eleven Southern states had *seceded* (separated or withdrawn) from the Union and formed the Confederacy. This plunged the nation into Civil War (1861–1865). During those painful, tragic years, Lincoln repeatedly used his amazing skill to help people understand what the war was about and to put into words what the nation was feeling.

He approached the issue of slavery with caution and wisdom. When he issued the Emancipation Proclamation in September 1862 (effective January 1, 1863), which freed the slaves, he applied it only to the states still in rebellion. He also helped people see that fighting to end slavery provided a noble cause in addition to preserving the Union.

Shopping Spree

Mary Todd Lincoln had grown up in a wealthy Southern family. One of her favorite pastimes was shopping. When she took up residence in the White House, she seemed to take that as an invitation to shop. Her spending sprees soon totaled $27,000, a huge sum in the 1860s. In the space of four months, she purchased three hundred pairs of gloves.

☆ ☆

Family Matters

The president and his wife seemed to have a happy marriage, until the many pressures on them during his presidency began to affect her mental stability. Mary Todd Lincoln had a brother and three half-brothers fighting for the Confederacy. This led some members of Congress to accuse her of being a Southern sympathizer or even a spy. In 1862, one of the Lincoln's sons, Willie, died, and the first lady began to act strangely. She was sitting next to her husband when he was assassinated. The death of another son, Tad, in 1871, seemed to finally push her over the edge. In 1875, she was declared insane. She died in 1882 at the home of her sister.

The Lincolns' oldest son, Robert Todd Lincoln, had a long career in government, serving as secretary of war for presidents Garfield and Arthur. He happened to be nearby when three presidents were assassinated: his father, James Garfield (1881), and William McKinley (1901). After McKinley's death, Robert Lincoln vowed never to appear in public with a president.

☆ ☆

In November 1863, in Lincoln's famous Gettysburg Address, his eloquent words persuaded many that the sacrifice of so many lives had been necessary. As the war drew to a close, some die-hard supporters of the Confederacy hatched a plot to assassinate the president and other key leaders. A brilliant but mentally unbalanced actor named John Wilkes Booth fatally wounded Lincoln while he was attending a play with his wife. The other parts of the conspiracy failed; Booth and others were killed or captured, tried, and hanged.

Word Detection

For each of the eight clues listed, write the correct answer, a five-letter word, in the blank spaces. To spell the word, you will use five of the six letters printed on the same line. Write the extra, or sixth, letter in the last column. When you've finished, unscramble the letters in the last column to find something we associate with Lincoln.

1 Talent   __ __ __ __ __   S L V L I K   __

2 Needed to elect   __ __ __ __ __   V T S E L O   __

3 Some made of logs   __ __ __ __ __   I B I N C A   __

4 Part of Congress   __ __ __ __ __   U S H E C O   __

5 Not a free man   __ __ __ __ __   I S V E A L   __

6 Where Lincoln failed   __ __ __ __ __   T R R E S O   __

7 Confederacy   __ __ __ __ __   S T W U O H   __

8 North   __ __ __ __ __   N O N I A U   __

Answers appear at the back of the book.

Mr. Lincoln's Stovepipe Hat

Lincoln stood 6 feet 4 inches tall, making him the tallest president. The stovepipe hat he often wore added several inches more. He also admitted that he often stuffed important papers in his hat and sometimes forgot where they were. You can use your stovepipe hat the same way.

 You'll Need

adult helper, if needed
piece of string
3 sheets of heavyweight black construction paper
scissors
ruler
white glue
paper clips
3 or 4 rubber bands
drawing compass

1 Use a piece of string to measure around your head for your hat size. This will provide the circumference (distance around) the top of the hat.

2 From a sheet of the black construction paper, cut a rectangle 10 to 12 inches high and 1 inch wider than your string measurement. Form the paper into a 12-inch-high tube with an overlap of ½ inch on the side.

3 Glue the side of the stovepipe, using the ½-inch overlap. Use paper clips at the top and bottom to hold the pieces until the glue dries. You can also slide rubber bands over the top for a better hold.

4 On another sheet of construction paper, draw a circle slightly larger than the string measurement. Draw another circle outside the first one that is 1 inch larger. Cut out the larger circle. We'll call this circle A.

5 On a third sheet of construction paper, copy the large circle. Then draw a still larger circle, about 4 inches larger, around the second circle. This will be circle B.

6 *For the top of the hat:* On circle A, draw and cut 6 V-shaped wedges, as shown. This will create 6 flaps to fold in. Glue the flaps to the inside of the stovepipe.

7 *For the brim:* Cut out circle B, and cut out the small inside circle. This will give you a doughnut-shaped piece for the brim. Draw, then cut out, 6 wedges from the inside of the doughnut. Fold these up and glue them to the inside of the stovepipe. Your stovepipe hat is now ready.

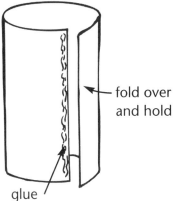

fold over and hold

glue

Circle A

cut out wedges

Circle B

cut out

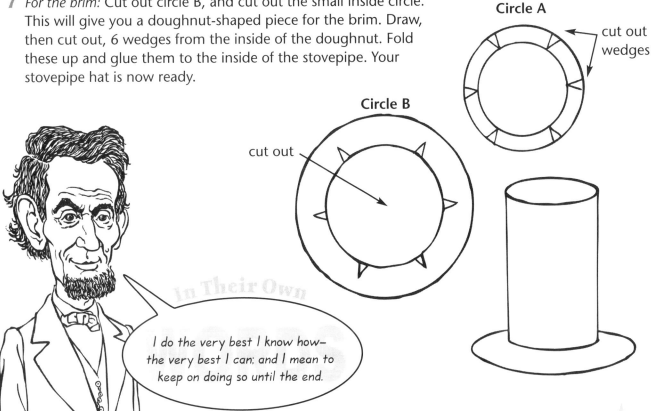

In Their Own

I do the very best I know how—the very best I can; and I mean to keep on doing so until the end.

ANDREW
JOHNSON

★ ★

Seventeenth President, 1865–1869

Born *December 29, 1808, Raleigh, North Carolina*
Died *July 31, 1875, Carter County, Tennessee*

☆ ☆ ☆ ☆ ☆ ☆ ☆ ☆ ☆ ☆

Johnson Firsts

In addition to being the first president to be impeached, Andrew Johnson was also the only president to have no formal schooling at all; the only president to become a senator after his term as president; and the first to receive an official visit from a queen (when Queen Emma of the Sandwich Islands—later Hawaii—visited the White House).

☆ ☆ ☆ ☆ ☆ ☆ ☆ ☆ ☆ ☆

Family Matters

When Johnson married Eliza McCardle, he was eighteen years old and she was sixteen. No other president and first lady had married so young. Eliza helped Johnson learn writing and math, and the couple had five children. She died about six months after her husband.

In 1861, a banner strung across the street of Greeneville, Tennessee, read, "Andrew Johnson, Traitor." Eight years later, after suffering the humiliation of impeachment (when a public official is accused of wrongdoing), a new banner welcomed him home with the words, "Andrew Johnson, Patriot." That sharp swing in opinion was typical of this man's life and career.

Born into a poor family in North Carolina, Andrew Johnson was apprenticed to a tailor instead of being sent to school. Even as a boy, he was both independent and stubborn. He ran away from his master and set up his own shop in Greeneville. He was soon making enough money to bring his mother and brothers and sisters to live with him. And he was popular enough in Greeneville to be elected mayor at the age of twenty-one.

Johnson struggled to learn to read and write. He also joined a debating club, gaining powerful skills in public speaking. His basic popularity carried him through a progression of elected offices: Tennessee legislature (1835–1843), House of Representatives (1843–1853), governor of Tennessee (1853–1857), and senator (1857–1862). Throughout these years, he stubbornly stuck to his principles, refusing to compromise on issues such as preserving the Union and supporting a homestead act that would enable the poor to become pioneer farmers.

In 1861, as the Union was divided by Civil War, Johnson struggled against Tennessee's secession. When the state did secede, Johnson became the only Southerner to remain in the Senate. This made him a hero in the North but a traitor at home. As Union forces gained control of Tennessee in 1862, President Lincoln appointed him military governor, a position he performed with fairness to both sides. As a reward for his loyalty, Johnson was made Lincoln's vice president in 1864. One month after he was sworn in, Johnson was thrust into the presidency by Lincoln's assassination.

As president, Johnson found himself involved in a controversy over plans for restoring the defeated Southern states to the Union. Johnson chose to follow Lincoln's plan for restoring the Union as quickly as possible. He issued a generous plan for amnesty (pardon) for the Southern states in May 1865. But some members of Congress were determined to punish the

South. They rejected Johnson's plan and restored military rule in the South in 1867. The president, in turn, defied an act of Congress by firing the secretary of war, and the House voted to impeach him for "high crimes and misdemeanors."

Johnson was put on trial before the Senate in May 1868, but the attempt to remove him from office failed by one vote. A year later, Johnson returned home to a hero's welcome. After several years of retirement, he was sent back to the Senate in 1875. Many people had come to admire Johnson's courage, and Congress erupted in cheers when he entered. But the one speech he gave was to be his last. He returned to Tennessee during a Senate recess, suffered a stroke, and died.

Pecan Pie

Here's a chance to try what was probably *the* favorite pie of nineteenth-century Southerners, including Andrew Johnson. Pecan pie is very rich. It's a good idea to serve it with a little whipped cream.

1 Have an adult preheat the oven to 450 degrees F.

2 Line the pie tin with the pie crust.

3 Break the eggs into a large bowl. Beat well with an egg beater or mixer.

4 Add the sugar, salt, vanilla, and corn syrup. Stir well with a wooden spoon.

5 Spread the pecans into the pie shell. Pour the egg mixture over the pecans.

6 Bake at 450 degrees F for 10 minutes. Reduce heat to 350 degrees F and bake for another 35 minutes.

7 Have an adult use oven mitts to remove the pie from the oven and place it on a cooling rack.

8 Serve at room temperature with whipped cream if desired.

Stuffed Calico Cat

Andrew Johnson had to be an expert with needle and thread when he was a tailor. Here's a fun sewing project for beginners.

1 Copy the drawing of the Calico Cat on a sheet of paper and cut it out.

2 Place 2 pieces of calico fabric with the print sides facing each other. Place the pattern on the calico, trace around it in pencil, and cut out the cat shape.

3 Pin the 2 pieces of fabric together, still with the print sides facing each other.

4 Sew all the way around the cat, about ¼ inch from the edge, but leave a 2-inch opening at the bottom. Place the stitches close together for a firm hold.

Change of Heart

The conspirators who planned the assassination of Lincoln also planned to kill Johnson and several members of the Cabinet. The man assigned to kill Johnson changed his mind at the last minute.

 **You'll Need**

3 eggs
½ cup sugar
¼ teaspoon salt
1 teaspoon vanilla
1 cup dark corn syrup
1½ cups chopped pecans
ready-made pie crust
ready-made whipped cream (optional)
adult helper
measuring cup
measuring spoon
9-inch pie tin
large bowl
egg beater or mixer
wooden spoon
oven mitts
cooling rack
Makes 6 to 8 servings

 **You'll Need**

sheet of paper and pencil
scissors
ruler
2 pieces of calico fabric (about 8 inches square)
10–12 straight pins
needle and thread to match fabric's basic color
cotton stuffing
scrap of yarn
fabric glue or white glue
scrap of ribbon

49

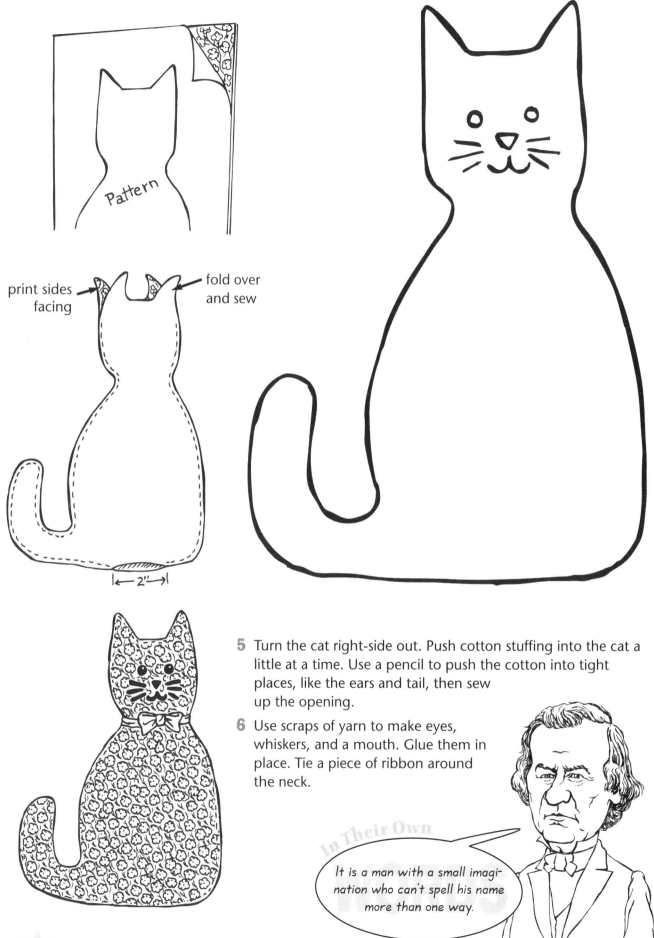

Pattern

print sides facing

fold over and sew

2"

5 Turn the cat right-side out. Push cotton stuffing into the cat a little at a time. Use a pencil to push the cotton into tight places, like the ears and tail, then sew up the opening.

6 Use scraps of yarn to make eyes, whiskers, and a mouth. Glue them in place. Tie a piece of ribbon around the neck.

In Their Own WORDS

It is a man with a small imagination who can't spell his name more than one way.

ULYSSES S. GRANT

Eighteenth President, 1869–1877

Born *April 27, 1822, Point Pleasant, Ohio*
Died *July 23, 1885, Mount McGregor, New York*

Up to the time that American unity was shattered by the opening shots of the Civil War in April 1861, Ulysses S. Grant had not been having a very successful career. He had resigned his army commission, then failed at farming and at selling real estate. He was trying to support a family of five on the salary of a store clerk. He was forty years old and felt like a failure. Over the next six years, however, Grant became the greatest hero the nation had seen since George Washington. He was to remain the most popular American for years to come, even after eight rocky years as president.

Growing up in rural Ohio, Grant, whose real given name was Hiram, worked on the family farm and developed great skill with horses. His father secured an appointment to West Point for him in 1843, and Grant struggled through four years with a mediocre record.

After serving bravely in the war with Mexico (1846–1848), he languished in remote, isolated posts, separated from his wife and growing family. He resigned his commission in 1854. After suffering through the years of failure, he was finally hired by his younger brothers to clerk in their store in Galena, Illinois.

The Civil War provided a new life for Grant. Given command of a regiment, he quickly proved that he was a brilliant battlefield leader. After winning crucial victories for the North at Forts Henry and Donelson, followed by taking the fortified city of Vicksburg, Grant was placed in command of all Union armies by Lincoln. Taking advantage of superior manpower and weaponry, he relentlessly advanced against the Confederate Army of General Robert E. Lee, forcing him to surrender in April 1865.

A grateful nation elected the war hero to the presidency in 1868 and reelected him in 1872. During Grant's second term, a number of scandals were exposed. Although the president was never involved, it was clear that he had surrounded himself with crooks who took advantage of his trust.

The same thing occurred after he left the White House. Once again, "friends" cheated him, and he found himself almost penniless while also battling terminal cancer. Through the friendship of Samuel Clemens (Mark Twain), Grant was able to publish his personal history only weeks before he died. The book provided a sizable fortune for his family and is still regarded as an outstanding military history.

☆☆☆☆☆☆☆☆☆☆

Family Matters

Ulysses Grant was a distant cousin of Grover Cleveland, the twenty-second and twenty-fourth president, and of Franklin D. Roosevelt, the thirty-second president.

Grant married Julia Dent after the war with Mexico, and she followed him faithfully to many of his army posts. Her faith was rewarded when Grant became famous, and she loved being the first lady. She and Grant had four children. She was buried with Ulysses in 1902.

☆☆☆☆☆☆☆☆☆☆

First Female Candidate

In 1872, Victoria Woodhull became the first woman to run for the presidency. Her vice-presidential candidate was Frederick Douglass, abolitionist and former slave. Susan B. Anthony tried to vote in that election, gaining publicity for the cause of women's suffrage (the right to vote).

Battlefield Strategy

Things You'll Need

2 players
4 sheets of graph paper or plain paper
ruler
2 pencils
copy machine, if available

Grant's Tomb

After Grant's death, about one hundred thousand people contributed to the building of Grant's Tomb, overlooking the Hudson River in New York City. It was dedicated in 1897. For the next thirty years, it was America's most popular monument, surpassing even the newly erected Statue of Liberty.

One of Grant's special battlefield skills was his brilliant use of artillery. Often the Civil War cannons were out of sight of the enemy, so a good general relied on scouts to report hits and misses. He could then try to adjust the next volley more accurately.

In the game of Battlefield Strategy, you can try to outmaneuver your opponent.

1 On graph paper or plain paper, use a ruler and pencil to make a grid of 144 squares: 12 across and 12 down. Write the letters A to L down the side and the numbers 1 to 12 across the top, as shown.

2 Copy the grids so that each player has 2 copies. If you can use a copy machine, run off multiple copies for future games. Each player labels one sheet as the Defense Grid and the other sheet as the Open-Fire Grid.

3 Each player has 5 military units. These can be placed anywhere the player wishes, making sure that the enemy does not see their location. The 5 units are 2 cavalry regiments (shade in 4 squares for each); 2 artillery regiments (3 squares); and 1 infantry regiment (2 squares). The drawing shows possible placement of the 5 regiments.

4 The object of the game is to knock out all of your enemy's regiments. Decide any way you wish who opens fire first. Player 1 fires a shot by announcing a square, such as C-4 or A-7. Player 2 checks his or her Defense Grid. If no part of a regiment has been hit, he or she says, "It's a miss." If the shot strikes a regiment, player 2 announces, "It's a hit!" and marks an X on that square. Player 1 marks his or her Open-Fire Grid for every shot—a dot for a miss, an X for a hit.

5 Player 1 fires a total of 10 shots. A regiment is knocked out of action when all of its squares have an X. When a player scores a hit, good strategy says to concentrate more shots in that area until a regiment is

Sample Placement Defense Grid

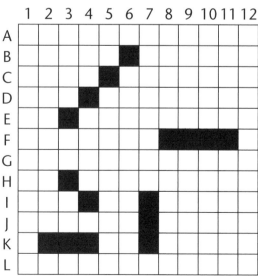

Sample Open-Fire Grid

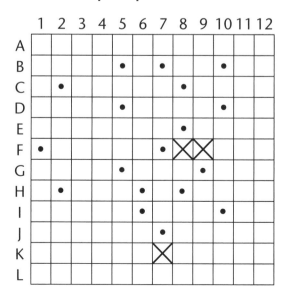

knocked out. The player in defense announces, "It's a hit, and one of my cavalry regiments is knocked out."

6 Each player takes turns firing 10 shots. But once a player has lost a regiment, his or her shots are reduced by two in the next round. So a player who has lost 3 regiments would fire only 4 shots in the next volley.

7 The battle is over when a player is forced to surrender because all of his or her regiments are out of action.

Independence Day Cupcakes

The nation celebrated its centennial in 1876, the one hundredth anniversary of the Declaration of Independence. President Grant presided over the biggest birthday party the country had ever seen—a six-month Centennial Exhibition in Philadelphia. Celebrations were held throughout the country, and red, white, and blue colors were everywhere.

In this activity, you can make your own Fourth of July cupcakes.

1 Have an adult preheat the oven to 350 degrees F.

2 Sift together the flour, baking powder, and salt into a small bowl.

3 Crack an egg into the other small bowl and beat thoroughly. In the large bowl, use an egg beater or mixer to cream the butter until light and fluffy. Gradually beat in the sugar, vanilla, and egg.

4 Stir in ½ cup of the flour mixture then ¼ cup milk.

5 Stir in another ½ cup of the flour mixture, and another ¼ cup milk.

6 Add the rest of the flour mixture, stir, and spoon into the cupcake tin lined with cupcake papers.

7 Put the cupcakes in the oven and bake for 20 to 25 minutes. Have an adult using oven mitts take the cupcakes out of the oven and put them on a cooling rack.

8 Place about ⅓ cup of the frosting in each of the two small dishes. Stir a little blue food coloring into one dish and red into the other.

9 When the cupcakes have cooled, use a table knife to spread the red, white, and blue frosting on them. You can top each cupcake with 1 color, or try using all 3 colors.

1½ cups all purpose flour
2 teaspoons baking powder
¼ teaspoon salt
1 egg
4 ounces unsalted butter at room temperature
¾ cup sugar
½ teaspoon vanilla
½ cup milk
1 cup white frosting
blue and red food coloring
adult helper
measuring cup
measuring spoon
sifter
2 small bowls
egg beater or mixer
large bowl
wooden spoon
cupcake tin
cupcake papers
oven mitts
cooling rack
2 small dishes (for coloring frosting)
teaspoon
table knife
MAKES 1 DOZEN CUPCAKES

It was my fortune, or misfortune, to be called to the office of chief executive without any previous political training.

RUTHERFORD B. HAYES

Nineteenth President, 1877–1881

Born *October 4, 1822, Delaware, Ohio*
Died *January 17, 1893, Fremont, Ohio*

In the 1876 presidential election, the issue people cared about most was honesty in government. For eight years, the Grant administration had been riddled with corruption, and although Grant remained enormously popular, voters demanded reform. Both Republican Rutherford B. Hayes and Democrat Samuel J. Tilden of New York were reform-minded governors with sparkling records. When the election was over, however, it was considered one of the most dishonest in history. To Democrats, Hayes only became president because of a "stolen" election.

Rutherford B. Hayes seemed the perfect candidate for the times. He was a vigorous, good-looking man, with a full beard and an easygoing, friendly manner. Graduating from Kenyon College and Harvard Law School, he volunteered for service in the Civil War. He had no military training, but he proved to be a natural leader and took part in fifty engagements. He was wounded four times and had his horse shot from under him four times.

When friends nominated him for Congress, he agreed to run but refused to campaign while still in uniform. He still won the election and took his seat after leaving service as a major general. Hayes served two terms in Congress, then was elected governor of Ohio in 1868, winning a third term in 1876. His terms as governor were so strictly honest that opponents called him Granny Hayes.

Hayes was exactly the candidate the Republicans needed in 1876, giving them a chance to escape the shadow of the Grant scandals. But when the votes were counted, it looked like Tilden was the winner. He had 4,284,040 votes while Hayes had 4,036,572. There was a problem in the Electoral College, however, when three Southern states sent in two slates of electoral votes, one set for each candidate. While Congress searched for a solution, the electoral votes stood 184 for Tilden, 165 for Hayes, with 185 needed to win.

☆☆☆☆☆☆☆☆☆☆☆

Family Matters

Hayes married Lucy Ware Webb in 1852. Over the years, they had eight children, although only five survived to adulthood. Both the president and the first lady were responsible for the decision not to serve alcohol in the White House. But the public gave the credit—or the blame—to Lucy. Since the most common substitute offered was lemonade, she became known as Lemonade Lucy.

The Women's Christian Temperance Union was so proud of Lucy that they had a full-length portrait painted of her. The portrait hangs in the White House.

☆☆☆☆☆☆☆☆☆☆☆

Famous Firsts

Hayes was the first president to use a telephone while in office. He was also the first to visit the West Coast while in office. And First Lady Lucy Ware Webb Hayes was the first president's wife to be a college graduate.

After more than three months of debate, Congress appointed a commission to settle the issue. The commission gave all 20 votes—and the presidency—to Hayes. Many Democrats claimed the election had been "stolen," but Tilden chose not to fight the decision.

During his term as president, Hayes did reform the civil service—the method for hiring government workers. Many political leaders disliked the new approach because they could no longer give jobs to their followers. They also cared little for the new White House ban on smoking and drinking. Few Democratic leaders were sorry when Hayes announced he would not seek nomination for reelection in 1880. He spent the last twelve years of his life in retirement.

Lucy's Lemonade

In the mid-1800s, people used solid cones of sugar, or loaf sugar. To make lemonade, they would break off lumps and rub them on lemon rinds "until they [sugar lumps] have imbibed all the oil from them [lemons]," then press the lemons and pour boiling water over it all. You can use a simpler method.

1 Roll the lemons on a cutting board with the flat of your hand. This allows the juice to flow more freely.

2 Have an adult help you cut the lemons in half. Squeeze out the juice and pour through a strainer into a pitcher or jug. Remove the pits from the strainer. You can add some or all of the pulp to the juice, depending on taste.

3 Add the sugar and the water to the juice. Stir vigorously until the sugar is blended in.

4 Chill until you're ready to serve. Add a small piece of lemon rind to each glass.

Things You'll Need

6 lemons
1 cup sugar
8 cups cold water
adult helper
cutting board
paring knife
juicer
strainer
pitcher or jug
wooden spoon
MAKES 8 GLASSES

Decorated Easter Eggs

Early in President Hayes's term, Congress announced that the traditional Easter Egg Roll could no longer be held on the fragile lawn of the Capitol. First Lady Lucy Hayes immediately announced that the White House would host the event in 1878, and it has been held there ever since.

In the mid-1800s, many people began using a wax-resist technique to make elaborate decorations on Easter eggs. You'll use a modified version of wax resist with wax crayons instead of beeswax.

1 With an adult's help, hard-boil the eggs: Place them in a 2-quart saucepan with enough water to cover them. Bring to a slow boil over medium heat, and continue a gentle boil for about 15 minutes.

2 While the eggs cook, plan several designs for your eggs on scrap paper. Keep in mind that the lines you draw with a white crayon will remain white. Try dots, squiggles, stripes, stars, or anything else you can think of for designs.

Things You'll Need

adult helper
6 fresh eggs
2-quart saucepan
tap water
scrap paper and pencil
white crayon
paper towels
Easter egg dye or food coloring—4 or 5 colors
4 or 5 plastic cups, 9-ounce size or larger
vinegar
teaspoon or stir stick
Easter basket
several sheets of newspaper
apron or smock

Worthy Opponent

Samuel J. Tilden (1814–1886) had achieved a great reform record as governor of New York and brought down the notorious Tweed Ring—a group of corrupt officials who controlled New York City politics for more than twenty years. After his death in 1886, his estate became the basis for the New York Public Library.

3 When the eggs are done, cool them under cold running water, then dry them with paper towels.

4 Draw a design on each egg with a white crayon.

5 Spread your work area with newspaper and wear a smock or apron.

6 Pour egg dye or food coloring in paper cups. Add tap water, according to directions on the egg-dye package, or, with food coloring, experiment with a few drops of color and vinegar in ¼ cup of water.

7 Place an egg with a white-crayon design in a cup of coloring. Use a teaspoon or stir stick to roll the egg around in the colored water. The longer the egg is in the dye, the deeper the color will be. The dye won't adhere to the white-crayon design.

8 Carefully lift the egg out of the dye. Let any coloring drip back into the cup. Place each colored egg on a paper towel to dry.

9 Repeat steps 6 and 7 with the other eggs.

10 When the eggs are dry, you can use the crayon to block off other areas to add a second color or even a third. Place your finished eggs in an Easter basket for display. Do not keep the eggs at room temperature for more than a few hours. If you plan to eat the eggs, it's best to keep them refrigerated.

Any officer fit for duty who at this crisis would abandon his post to electioneer . . . ought to be scalped.

JAMES A.
GARFIELD

* *

Twentieth President, 1881

Born *November 19, 1831, Orange, Ohio*
Died *September 19, 1881, Eberon, New Jersey*

James Abram Garfield was one of several presidents to have been born in a log cabin, rising from poverty and obscurity to attain the nation's highest office. Although his presidency lasted only a few months, people had high hopes that he could heal the divisions in his own party and in the nation.

His father died when Garfield was an infant, and his mother struggled to hold the family together. Garfield worked odd jobs, picked up education in different schools, and somehow blossomed as a scholar and a public speaker. He attended Western Reserve Eclectic (later Hiram College), then Williams College in Massachusetts, graduating in 1856. He taught at Hiram for a few years and then became its president.

Garfield's strong voice and persuasive speaking helped to shape his career. Throughout his years in college, he was a popular part-time minister. In 1859, his speaking skill led the Ohio governor to appoint him to fill a seat in the state senate.

His budding political career was interrupted by the Civil War. As a volunteer officer, he displayed unusual skill and courage, rising to the rank of major general. Garfield was elected to Congress in 1862, even though he refused to campaign or to take his seat until he finished his army service. In December 1863, he resigned his commission and took his seat in the House of Representatives. He served through eight more terms, until 1880, becoming one of the most powerful figures in Congress.

The 1880 election, pitting Garfield against Democrat Winfield Hancock, another war hero, was one of the closest in history. The final totals: Garfield had 4,454,416 votes (48.3 percent); Hancock had 4,444,952 (48.2 percent).

Garfield's presidency started out well. He healed many of the divisions within the Republican Party. Many people predicted that he would be the most popular president in history. But in July 1881, after only four months in office, Garfield was on his way to a vacation on the New Jersey shore when he was shot and fatally wounded by a lone assassin. The man was mentally disturbed and began stalking the president when he was refused a political appointment. Garfield clung to life for ninety days before he died in September 1881.

Special Skills

Garfield was left-handed, but he could write with both hands—at the same time. A favorite trick was to write in Latin with one hand while writing in Greek with the other.

Accident Prone

As a boy, Garfield often became so lost in thought while working that he suffered accidents. Several times, while working on the family farm, he cut himself with an ax. When he was sixteen, he worked on a canal boat, usually leading the horses along the tow path. In the space of six weeks, he fell into the canal fourteen times. Since Garfield couldn't swim, it was fortunate that the water was shallow.

The One and Only One

The name GARFIELD is hidden in the puzzle one time and only one time. It will read left to right; right to left; or up, down, or on the diagonal. When you find it, draw a line around it.

```
F R A G F L D R G E I L D F G E A R R L
R G F A L L I R F E D R G F I D E L A R
A L I F R G E F R I E D D I E L L R F G
D R F G E I L D F A I F G A R F D L E A
R A L E I F A L G D L E I F R A G F A L
G A R L F D E I L I A G D E G R I L E D
R G L I E D R F G E I L R G D E L A I E
D L E I G R A F I D R E F I L D A G E R
```

Jam Tea Tarts

After hearing a lecture by the great essayist Ralph Waldo Emerson, Garfield became devoted to a life of literature and self-improvement. His wife shared his passion for books. During their years in Washington, their favorite pastime was an evening of reading accompanied by tea and cookies or small cakes like the Jam Tea Tarts you'll make in this recipe.

1 Have an adult preheat the oven to 350 degrees F.

2 Place the butter and sugar in a large bowl. Cream these ingredients with a wooden spoon or an electric mixer until they are blended and fluffy.

3 Mix the flour and salt in a separate large bowl. Add the butter mixture and stir well until it forms a thick dough.

4 Break off bits of dough and form them with your hands into 1-inch balls.

5 Place the balls on a baking sheet about 1 inch apart. Press a well in the center of each tart and spoon a little jam (about ¼ teaspoon) into the well.

6 Bake the tarts for about 10 minutes. Have an adult using oven mitts remove the baking sheet from the oven and put the tarts on a cooling rack.

In Their Own WORDS

The elevation of the Negro race from slavery to the full rights of citizenship is the most important political change we have known since the adoption of the Constitution.

☆☆☆☆☆☆☆☆☆☆☆

Family Matters

Garfield married Lucretia Rudolph in 1858. The couple had seven children, two of whom died when they were young. Lucretia carefully researched the history of the White House, planning to restore it to its former glory. Before she could launch the project, however, she was stricken with malaria. President Garfield was on his way to be with her when he was shot. Lucretia survived her illness and lived for another thirty-six years.

☆☆☆☆☆☆☆☆☆☆☆

Things You'll Need

1 cup (2 sticks) unsalted butter at room temperature
⅓ cup sugar
1¾ cups all-purpose flour
pinch of salt
¼ cup jam—any flavor
adult helper
measuring cup
2 large bowls
wooden spoon
mixer
baking sheet
teaspoon
oven mitts
cooling rack
Makes about 18 tarts

Chester A. Arthur

Twenty-first President, 1881–1885

Born *October 5, 1829, Fairfield, Vermont*
Died *November 18, 1886, New York, New York*

Historians have often noted that the presidency can change a person in sudden and dramatic ways. No one reveals this more clearly than Chester A. Arthur. After a career as a political "boss," dispensing jobs in return for favors, Arthur became a serious and dignified president, dedicated to improving the government.

Chester Arthur was the son of a fiery preacher, living in northern Vermont and Upstate New York. His father provided his early education. "Chet" graduated from Union College in 1848 and taught part-time while studying law.

After several years in law practice, he served as a quartermaster during the Civil War, providing food and equipment for the Union armies. He was also active in Republican Party politics. In 1871, President Grant appointed him collector of the Port of New York. He used this post as the center of political patronage (jobs for favors) in the city and state, dispensing jobs to the party faithful. Arthur and Senator Roscoe Conklin ran the New York political machine, the most powerful in the country.

In 1880, Arthur was nominated for the vice presidency in the hope of unifying the Republican Party. Less than a year after the election of the Garfield-Arthur ticket, the assassination of Garfield thrust Chester Arthur into the presidency. The entire country was shocked. They couldn't believe that the most corrupt New York politician would soon be in charge of the country.

President Arthur surprised everyone. He refused to appoint Conklin or any of the party bosses to government posts and pushed civil service reform through Congress. Civil service exams replaced political patronage.

The president also restored dignity and civility to the White House. At 6 feet 2 inches tall and 225 pounds, Arthur was a big, friendly man and a great storyteller. Elegant White House dinners were an almost nightly occurrence, and he had the building completely redecorated, with greatly expanded greenhouses to satisfy his passion for flowers. By the end of his term, most Americans agreed with Mark Twain, who wrote, "It would be hard to better President Arthur's administration."

☆☆☆☆☆☆☆☆☆☆

Family Matters

Arthur married Ellen "Nell" Lewis Herndon in 1859. In 1880, shortly before his election to the vice presidency, she died of pneumonia, and Arthur was grief-stricken for months. Once he was in the White House, he had fresh flowers placed below her portrait every day. His younger sister, Mary, served as "Mistress of the House" for White House functions. The Arthurs had three children, but one boy died when he was only two.

☆☆☆☆☆☆☆☆☆☆

Elegant Arthur

Chester Arthur loved to dress in the height of fashion. People called him Elegant Arthur. He reportedly owned eighty pairs of pants and often changed several times in a day. He also enjoyed shopping at the best tailors and once bought twenty-five suits in a single day.

Arthur's defiance of his own Republican Party ruined his chances to be nominated for president in 1884. But he had already said he would not run. He knew but told no one that he was suffering from a terminal illness. He died a few months after leaving office.

Paper "Stained Glass" Design

Louis Comfort Tiffany enjoyed an extraordinary career that extended from the 1870s through the 1920s. Many of his designs for the White House in Chester A. Arthur's time were later considered too dark or overwhelming and were removed. An elegant stained glass screen in the entrance hall remained and is considered one of Tiffany's masterpieces. In this project, you can make your own version of a Tiffany design.

1 Draw a geometric design, like the one shown here, on a piece of paper. Experiment until you have a design you like. The lines on your drawing should be wide, between $\frac{1}{4}$ and $\frac{1}{2}$ inch wide, because the tissue paper will be glued to the back of those lines.

2 Copy the design on the sheet of black construction paper. Place the design on a cutting board and have an adult cut out all the open spaces with a craft knife.

3 Choose the tissue paper colors you want for one of the sections. Cut the tissue paper a little larger than the opening. Spread a little glue on the back of the construction paper framing that section. Place the tissue paper over the opening and press it in place.

4 Repeat step 3 for all of the openings. Alternate colors any way you wish.

5 Hang your Tiffany design in a sunny window.

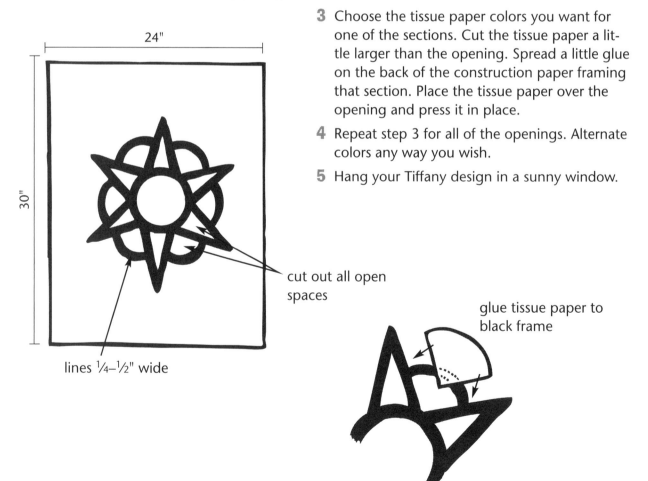

24"

30"

cut out all open spaces

lines $\frac{1}{4}$–$\frac{1}{2}$" wide

glue tissue paper to black frame

Blow-Up Party Invitations

In 1883, President Arthur's twelve-year-old daughter, Ellen "Nellie" Arthur, hosted the first White House Christmas party for needy children. To make invitations for any kind of party, try this project idea created by a young woman in Chicago in about 1890.

1 Blow up a balloon about three-quarters of its largest size. Tie the end closed with a knot that will be easy to untie.

2 With the felt-tip pen, write your invitation on the balloon: day, time, place, what or who the party is for, and any other necessary information. Gently rest the balloon on your work surface to make writing easier.

3 Let the air out of the balloon, and place it in a stamped, addressed envelope. Continue with the rest of the balloons. Seal the envelopes before mailing.

You'll Need

medium-size balloon for each invitation

felt-tip pen, medium or fine tip, any color

stamp for each invitation

envelope for each invitation

The Tiffany Touch

Arthur refused to move into the White House until it was completely redecorated. He had twenty-four wagonloads of furniture and junk removed and sold at auction. The redecorating was in the hands of Louis Comfort Tiffany, famed for his stained glass windows, lamp shades, and other items.

In Their Own Words

I may be President of the United States, but my private life is nobody's business.

Grover Cleveland

**Twenty-second President, 1885–1889;
Twenty-fourth President, 1893–1897**

Born *March 18, 1837, Caldwell, New Jersey*
Died *June 24, 1908, Princeton, New Jersey*

The deep divisions in America that had lingered since the Civil War seemed to end with Grover Cleveland's election in 1888. In fact, he was the first president since Lincoln who had not been an army officer. He became noted for his great honesty, even when that honesty turned important party leaders against him.

Born in New Jersey, Grover Cleveland was four years old when his father, a minister, moved the family to a small town in western New York. Even as a boy, Cleveland was dedicated to honesty and hard work: "If we expect to be great and good men," he wrote in an essay at age nine, "and be respected and esteemed by our friends, we must improve . . . when we are young."

When he was sixteen, Cleveland moved to Buffalo, where he worked and studied law. He entered law practice in 1859 and became active in local politics. After serving as sheriff, he was elected mayor of Buffalo. He had been mayor only a year when his ambitious reforms persuaded voters to elect him governor of New York (1883–1885). In his reform of civil service hiring, he lived up to his slogan, "Public office is a public trust."

As the Democrats' reform candidate in 1884, Cleveland defeated Republican James G. Blaine of Maine, receiving 49 percent of the popular vote to 48 percent for Blaine in another close nineteenth-century election. Cleveland was the first Democrat in the White House in more than twenty-four years, and party leaders were eager to make sweeping changes. But they didn't count on the new president's insistence on honesty and integrity. He vetoed (rejected) 413 bills in his first term (584 for two terms)—more than all twenty-one previous presidents combined.

Cleveland's insistence on honest government helped him retain his popularity, even though several party leaders turned against him. In 1888, he lost the election to Benjamin Harrison, but the Democrats nominated him again in 1892. This time he beat Harrison, becoming the only president to serve two terms not in consecutive order.

☆☆☆☆☆☆☆☆☆☆☆☆☆☆☆☆☆☆☆☆☆☆

Family Matters

After one year in office, Cleveland became the first president to be married in the White House when he married his ward, twenty-one-year-old Frances Folsom. He showed his penchant for hard work by writing out the wedding invitations himself and continuing to work on the day of the wedding. Frances was the daughter of Cleveland's law partner. He had known her all her life and had even bought her her first baby carriage. After her father died, Cleveland took charge of her inheritance and her education.

The public and the press were so eager for information about the first lady that their honeymoon became a nightmare of pressing crowds and reporters with binoculars, telescopes, and cameras. Cleveland was so furious at the press that he never again gave an interview. The Clevelands had five children: three girls and two boys. When the Clevelands left the White House after his first term, the first lady told the staff, "I want everything just the way it is now when we come back. That will be exactly four years from now."

☆☆☆☆☆☆☆☆☆☆☆☆☆☆☆☆☆☆☆☆☆☆

Cleveland's second term was marred by his inability to handle two important issues: a deep economic recession (business downturn) and the growing conflict between business owners and labor unions. In spite of these problems, historians voted Cleveland one of six "near-great" presidents.

The Baby Ruth Candy Bar Myth

In the 1920s, the Williamson Candy Company announced a new candy bar: the *Baby Ruth*. Many people thought it was named after Ruth Cleveland, who was known as Baby and who had been immensely popular with the public. Many others thought the name honored baseball great Babe Ruth. The president of the company exploded both myths when he explained that the candy bar was named after his granddaughter.

Sock Hand Puppet

With three of the five Cleveland children sharing the White House during Cleveland's terms, the living quarters had an unusual display of toys for tots, including easy-to-make toys like these hand puppets made out of socks.

 **You'll Need**

clean old sock for each puppet
pencil
needle and thread
buttons, beads, scraps of ribbon
craft glue
scraps of fabric

1 Place a sock over your hand and use a pencil to mark where features will be: eyes, nose, mouth, ears. Your puppets might be comical people or animals.

2 With a needle and thread, sew button eyes on the sock. You can use craft glue to attach some features, like scrap yarn for a nose and a mouth.

3 Fabric scraps work well for things like a puppy's ears. You can use felt for kittens' ears that need to stand up.

Build a Word

Figure out the clues to find the seven words or names, and write your answers in the spaces. One is done for you. The letters in the squares will form an eighth word, but it's scrambled. Unscramble it to find someone close to the president.

1 Cleveland's top spot in New York State

1 G O V E R N O R

2 The chief executive

2 _ _ _ _ _ _ _ _ _

3 Beat Cleveland in 1888

3 _ _ _ _ _ _ _

4 Where Frances and Grover married

4 _ _ _ _ _ _ _ _ _ _

5 Local law enforcement officer

5 _ _ _ _ _ _ _

6 Where Cleveland spent a year as mayor

6 _ _ _ _ _ _ _

7 A city in Ohio and a president

7 _ _ _ _ _ _ _ _

8 _ _ _ _ _ _ _

Answers appear at the back of the book.

What's the use of being elected or reelected unless you stand for something?

BENJAMIN

HARRISON

Twenty-third President, 1889–1893

Born *August 20, 1822, North Bend, Ohio*
Died *March 13, 1901, Indianapolis, Indiana*

The troops in Benjamin Harrison's Civil War regiment affectionately called him Little Ben, and at 5 feet 6 inches, he was America's second-shortest president. But he had all the stature needed to win the presidency in 1888. "Grandfather's hat fits!" he declared, referring to William Henry Harrison, the ninth president.

When Benjamin Harrison made up his mind about something, he moved swiftly and decisively. By the time he was twenty-one, he had graduated from college. He earned his law degree after two more years of study, married, and moved from the family's Ohio home to Indianapolis. After establishing a successful law practice, he volunteered for service in the Civil War, leading an Indiana regiment for three years and rising to the rank of brigadier general.

Harrison made his first foray into politics in 1876, losing a close race for governor. Campaigning did not come easily to him. He seemed so stiff and formal that he became known as the "human iceberg." Although he never overcame his distaste for small talk, his campaigning was aided by the fact that he was one of the most gifted public speakers of the late 1800s.

In 1880, Harrison was elected to the Senate. In 1888, he was elected president by a majority of Electoral College votes, even though he trailed Grover Cleveland in the popular vote by 100,000. His four years in the White House were mediocre. His most significant act was a campaign to give greater importance to the American flag. At a New York celebration of his inauguration that occurred on the centennial of George Washington's inauguration as the first president, Harrison urged that the Stars and Stripes be flown over every schoolhouse, post office, and public building in the country. The idea spread rapidly, and the flag became a fixture in every community.

Family Matters

Benjamin's father, John Scott Harrison, had the distinction of being the only man who was the son of one president and the father of another. John Scott Harrison was a member of Congress from Wyoming for two terms in the 1850s. Benjamin Harrison's grandson William was also a congressman, representing Wyoming a century after his great-grandfather!

Benjamin married Caroline Lavinia Scott in 1853. While young Caroline was a student in a women's college, Harrison came to see her so many evenings that the women called him "that pious moonlight dude." Benjamin and Caroline had one son and one daughter. Caroline died in 1892, and Harrison later married a widow, Mary Dimmick, who was Caroline's niece. Benjamin and Mary had one daughter.

Harrison's bid for reelection in 1892 failed, but he was not sorry to leave the presidency. "The repugnance to further public service," he said, "deepens within me every day." He renewed his law practice and gained a reputation for brilliance in international law. Harrison died suddenly of pneumonia in 1901.

Detecting Electric Charges

The Harrisons were not the only people to be either frightened of electricity or fascinated by it. When the first electric lights were installed in a New York City department store, people stayed away because they were afraid of an explosion.

Throughout the late 1800s, people developed a great variety of devices to help them understand how electricity worked. Many of these devices were called *electroscopes*. You'll make one version of an electroscope in this project.

1 Push the wire (or straightened paper clip) all the way through the cork so that only about ½ inch sticks up above the cork. Make a little hook or L at the bottom of the wire.

2 Cut a strip of aluminum foil about 3 inches long and 1 inch wide. Fold the strip in half. Cut a notch at the fold so that the 2 halves are held together by a very narrow strip. Hang the strip from the wire hook.

3 Gently insert the cork into the jar and press it to seal the jar.

4 Rub the comb vigorously across the wool, then touch the comb to the bit of wire above the cork. Rub it back and forth on the wire for 1 or 2 seconds. You will see the 2 halves of foil move apart.

5 Now touch the wire with your finger. The 2 halves will move back together.

How the electroscope works: Rubbing the comb with the piece of wool makes the comb become electrically charged. When an electrically charged object (the comb) touches the metal wire, the metal conducts the charge to the aluminum. Both halves receive the same charge, so they repel each other and fly apart. When a finger touches the metal, the charge "leaks" out and the two halves go back.

Things You'll Need

6-inch piece of copper wire (substitute a paper clip if necessary)

bottle or jar with a cork stopper (*Note:* Many different bottles and jars can be fitted with a cork. If possible, use a jar with a cork that's at least 1½ inches in diameter.)

scissors

aluminum foil

comb

piece of wool or silk, like a scarf

Holiday Chain

First Lady Caroline Harrison installed the first White House Christmas tree. You can use this traditional popcorn-and-cranberry chain to decorate a Christmas tree. Or, for any holiday, drape it around a doorway, mirror, or plant. Make it a postholiday gift for birds, too.

1 Pop the popcorn, and leave it in an uncovered bowl until it becomes stale.

2 Push thread through the eye of the needle. You can leave the end of the thread attached to the spool.

3 Carefully push the needle through a piece of popcorn or a cranberry. A thimble may help you avoid pricking your finger.

4 Keep on threading, alternating cranberries and popcorn.

5 When you have a long chain, cut the thread at the spool and tie the ends together in a firm knot. Your holiday chain is ready to use.

Things You'll Need

package of microwave popcorn
large bowl
needle and thread
package of fresh cranberries (about 1 pound)
thimble (optional)
scissors

Fear of the Dark?

In 1891, the Thomas Edison Company installed the first electric lights in the White House. For months, the president and First Lady Caroline Harrison slept with the lights on all night. The reason was not fear of the dark but fear of getting a shock if they touched the switch, so they waited for the engineer to come in the morning to shut off the lights.

It is quite as illogical to despise a man because he is rich as because he is poor.

WILLIAM McKINLEY

Twenty-fifth President, 1897–1901

Born *January 19, 1843, Niles, Ohio*
Died *September 14, 1901, Buffalo, New York*

Perhaps no president was more beloved in his time than William McKinley. He was exceptionally kind and made friends easily. Even his opponents found him easy to like. He always knew what he wanted to do. "I have never been in doubt," he said, "since I was old enough to think intelligently, that I would some day be made president."

McKinley grew up in a small town in Ohio. His college education was interrupted by the Civil War. He served four years in an Ohio regiment commanded by Colonel Rutherford B. Hayes, the future president, rising from private to major. Although Hayes called him "one of the bravest and finest officers in the army," McKinley developed an intense hatred for war.

After the war, McKinley earned his law degree, established a practice, and entered politics. He was elected to the House of Representatives in 1876 and remained until 1891, except for one two-year gap. Elected governor of Ohio in 1892 and reelected two years later, he became known for his fairness, including support for labor unions in their struggles against giant corporations. While governor of Ohio, McKinley began a one-man campaign to let people know that he was "available" for the Republican nomination for the presidency, writing as many as three hundred letters a day.

It worked, and he was nominated for the presidency in 1896. He ran against Democrat William Jennings Bryan. McKinley won by a comfortable margin and defeated Bryan again in 1900. McKinley was helped by the country's energetic recovery from an economic recession, enabling the Republicans to promise "A Full Dinner Pail" in their campaign slogan.

The key event of McKinley's presidency was the Spanish-American War in 1898. For several years, Americans had become increasingly outraged by the way Spain governed nearby Cuba. In spite of his distaste for war, McKinley felt driven to it by public opinion and by Congress. The Spanish-American War was over in a few months, ending in an American victory that brought control of Spain's former colonies: Cuba, Puerto Rico, and the Philippines. Many Americans opposed keeping those possessions, but McKinley felt it was the only solution, and the United States became a colonial power.

Following his 1900 reelection, McKinley was in Buffalo for the 1901 Pan-American Exposition when he was shot by a lone assassin, an *anarchist* (person who is opposed to all government). McKinley died eight days later, on September 14, 1901.

The "Front-Porch Campaign"

When McKinley ran for the presidency, he remained at his home in Canton, Ohio. He ran what the press called the "front-porch campaign," speaking to groups brought in by the Republican Party. He did not want to leave his wife, Ida, because of her illness. During the campaign, he became the first to use campaign buttons.

The Highest Mountain

The tallest mountain in the United States was named after the president. Mount McKinley in Alaska is 20,320 feet above sea level.

Family Matters

McKinley and First Lady Ida McKinley were a very attractive couple. The talk of Washington was his loving attention to her as she became increasingly affected by a form of epilepsy. At White House dinners, he broke with tradition by having her sit next to him rather than at the far end of the table. If she started to have a seizure, he would gently place a handkerchief over her face until it passed, then continue as if nothing had happened.

Campaign Buttons

Things You'll Need

drawing compass or any small, round object
pencil
scrap of cardboard
scissors
construction paper or small photograph
white glue
felt-tip pen—any color
safety pin

Since William McKinley's run for the presidency produced the first campaign buttons, the device has been used for countless politicians and for all sorts of causes. You can create your own campaign buttons to promote yourself or a cause in which you believe.

1 Use a drawing compass or any small, round object to draw a small circle (2–3 inches in diameter) on a scrap of cardboard. Cut out the circle.

2 Cut a piece of construction paper the same size and glue it to the cardboard. If you prefer, you can cut a photograph to fit the circle or part of it.

3 Use a felt-tip pen to print a slogan or other message on the front of the button.

4 Glue a safety pin to the back, and your campaign button is ready for your promotional work.

Chile Con Carne

Things You'll Need

1 pound lean ground beef
medium onion, chopped
garlic clove, minced
two 14½-ounce cans diced or stewed tomatoes
two 15½-ounce cans red kidney beans
1 teaspoon salt
½ teaspoon pepper
1½ teaspoons chili powder
½ cup shredded cheddar cheese (optional)
adult helper
measuring cup
measuring spoon
cutting board
paring knife
large, deep skillet
wooden spoon
soup bowls
Makes 4 to 6 servings

American soldiers and sailors returned from the Spanish-American War with a taste for zesty Hispanic recipes. One dish, which became known as chile con carne (chile with meat), had been concocted less than twenty years earlier in the West Indies. You can add to the heat of the dish—or reduce it—by adjusting the chili powder.

1 With an adult's help, sauté the ground beef in a large skillet over medium-high heat until brown and crumbly. Drain off the fat.

2 Add the onion and garlic to the skillet and cook until soft.

3 Stir in the tomatoes, beans, salt, pepper, and chili powder.

4 Simmer over low heat for 50 minutes. Stir occasionally.

5 Serve warm. Sprinkle each bowl with shredded cheese, if desired.

War should never be entered upon until every agency of peace has failed.

THEODORE ROOSEVELT

Twenty-sixth President, 1901–1909

Born October 27, 1858, New York, New York
Died January 6, 1919, Oyster Bay, New York

The White House—and the nation—had never witnessed anyone like Teddy Roosevelt in the presidency. He was a virtual whirlwind of activity from 1901 to 1909. Everything he did seemed to be at a speeded-up pace, and most people loved every day of his action-packed presidency. Even those who opposed him were never bored.

Roosevelt was born in 1858 into one of New York's leading families. He was so puny and sickly as a boy that his father warned him he could never have a "useful career." With fierce determination Roosevelt built up his body through physical activity that became a way of life. As an adult, he preached the "strenuous" life. He boxed, swam, played tennis (once playing ninety-one games in a day), hiked, rode horses, and hunted, all with an energy and enthusiasm that wore out everyone around him. He still found time to read two or three books a day and to write twenty-four, including outstanding works on naval history, ranching, the settling of the West, and North American wildlife.

After graduating from Harvard in 1880, Roosevelt started climbing the New York political ladder. When his wife, Alice, died in childbirth in 1884, on the same day his mother died, he worked through his grief by spending two years as a rancher in Dakota Territory.

Roosevelt returned to New York in 1886, remarried, and leaped back into politics. He managed to make his positions on the Civil Service Commission and the New York City Police Commission seem like exciting news to reporters. Appointed assistant secretary of the navy, he helped build enthusiasm for war with Spain, and when war came, he resigned to form his own cavalry regiment, the Rough Riders. He came home from the war a hero for leading a charge up San Juan Hill in Cuba.

When McKinley ran for a second term, Roosevelt accepted the vice presidency, and a few months later when McKinley was assassinated, he became the nation's youngest president. As president, he led the nation in an important new direction: for the first time, the federal government accepted responsibility for the welfare of the people.

Family Matters

Teddy had one child, Alice, by his first wife, who died in 1886. Teddy then married a childhood friend, Edith Carow, and the two had five children of their own: Theodore, Kermit, Ethel, Archibald, and Quentin. The Roosevelt children were called "the White House Gang" by reporters. The children maintained a small menagerie at the White House, which included a total of nine dogs: Slippers, a cat with six toes on one paw; a horned toad; several guinea pigs; a blue Brazilian macaw named Eli Yale; a bear named Jonathan Edward, later given to the Washington zoo; a badger; and two ponies. When Archie was sick with measles, two brothers smuggled a pony up the White House elevator to visit him.

Teddy's Namesake Bear

On a hunting trip, President Roosevelt refused to shoot a bear because it was a cub. Reporters and cartoonists had fun with this reluctance, and Morris Michton created a cuddly stuffed bear as a child's toy. This first teddy bear is on display at the Smithsonian Institution in Washington, D.C.

 **Things You'll Need**

scissors
2 pieces of construction paper—any color
ruler
pencil
masking tape
4 pieces of white paper, 8½ × 11 inches
hole punch
narrow ribbon or yarn
crayon or felt-tip pen—any color

Roosevelt attacked giant corporations for destroying competition. He pressed Congress to pass legislation to protect Americans from unsafe foods and medicines. He transferred 125 million acres of land to forest reserve and made huge increases in the number of national parks and wildlife refuges. He even found time to become the first American to be awarded the Nobel Peace Prize for helping negotiate an end to the Russo-Japanese War.

Roosevelt was sorry to leave the presidency in 1909. "I will confess to you confidentially that I like the job," he said. He tried a comeback in 1912 by forming the Progressive, or "Bull Moose," Party, but he succeeded only in dividing the Republican Party, which enabled Democrat Woodrow Wilson to win. In retirement he found action in big-game hunting. He was disappointed that he couldn't be involved in World War I (1914–1918). Weakened by malaria he had contracted in Brazil, Roosevelt died quietly in his sleep in 1919.

Nature Sketchbook

At the age of nine, Roosevelt wrote his first "scholarly" paper: "The Natural History of Insects." This work was based on his own observations accompanied by sketches of several "carcasses." Here is an easy way to make your own nature sketchbook.

1 Make a cover for your sketchbook by cutting 2 pieces of construction paper, each measuring 6 by 9 inches.

2 To make a binding for the cover, measure a 1-inch-wide strip on the short side of each cover. Cut off the 2 strips, then tape each strip back in place with masking tape. Turn the covers over so that the tape is on the inside.

3 Cut the 4 pieces of white paper in half. Stack the 8 pages between the covers. Use the hole punch to make 4 holes through the binding strip and the pages.

4 Thread ribbon or yarn through the holes and tie bows.

5 Decorate the cover with a title, your name, sketches, or anything you want.

6 Use your sketchbook to draw pictures of birds, bugs, or other things in nature.

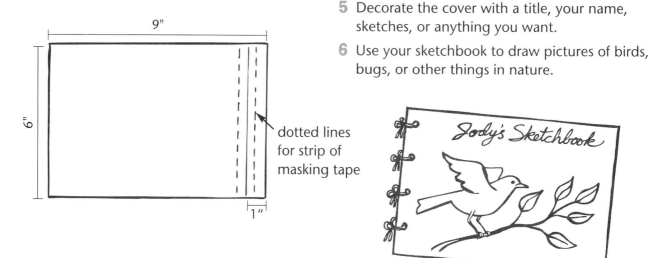

dotted lines for strip of masking tape

Word Search

Theodore Roosevelt was always busy. The following puzzle contains ten words associated with things that kept him busy. See if you can find and draw a line around all ten. Remember that the words can be read from left to right, right to left, up, down, or on a diagonal.

HIKING	TENNIS	READ	BOXING
SWIM	SPEECH	RANCH	HORSEBACK
WRITING	RIDE		

```
W H N T R E A X T R W I
A T E N N I S R N H K L
R D L U H R P H O U K S
A B E L T W E R A N C H
S R O A G N E A R T A E
X H C X N E C W D X B A
K D R M I W H R I D E M
I N S L K N A E B A S P
W R I T I N G H E W R L
B A M L H A C S I N O T
N R L R W N K M E A H I
H S E K B X A W R B S M
```

Answers appear at the back of the book.

Body Armor

On October 14, 1912, Roosevelt was on his way to deliver a speech in Milwaukee when a deranged German immigrant shot him in the chest. The bullet passed through the folded pages of his speech, then through an eyeglass case, and finally into the chest four inches, where it broke a rib. Roosevelt insisted on delivering his hour-long speech in his bloody shirt before going to the hospital. "I am going to make that speech if I die doing it," he said.

Get action; be sane; don't fritter away your time; create, act, take a place and be somebody; get action.

WILLIAM HOWARD
TAFT

★ ★

Twenty-seventh President, 1909–1913

Born *September 15, 1857, Cincinnati, Ohio*
Died *March 8, 1930, Washington, D.C.*

Family Matters

Taft married Helen "Nellie" Herron in 1886. They had three children, Robert, Helen, and Charles. Nellie Taft made a lasting contribution to Washington when she arranged to have three thousand Japanese cherry trees planted around the tidal basin. In a 1912 ceremony, Mrs. Taft and the wife of the Japanese ambassador planted the first few trees. While some of the trees had to be replaced, about one quarter of the original trees still survive and make for a colorful display of spring blossoms.

illiam Howard Taft was a big, jovial man and certainly the largest of our presidents at 6 feet 2 inches tall and 350 pounds. He was always well liked and enjoyed life enormously, even showing remarkable agility in baseball and tennis and on the dance floor. The only unhappy period in his life was his term as president.

Taft grew up in Cincinnati, Ohio. He was already bulky as a youth but a good athlete and an excellent student, always near the top of his class, including at Yale University and in law school at the University of Cincinnati. From 1880 to 1900, he held various court-related positions, including justice of the U.S. Court of Appeals. His lifelong dream was to be a justice on the Supreme Court.

After the United States gained control of the Philippines following the Spanish-American War (1898), the islands were torn by rebellion and corruption. President McKinley sent Taft to create order. He served as commissioner and then governor general from 1900 to 1904. Praised for his evenhanded treatment of the issues, he was chosen by President Roosevelt to be his secretary of war.

Taft became Roosevelt's friend and close ally. Roosevelt once said that he never worried about being away from Washington because "Taft is sitting on the lid." Taft twice turned down the Supreme Court to stay at Roosevelt's side, and then he agreed to run for the presidency in 1908.

Taft easily won the presidency and worked hard to continue Roosevelt's policies. He actually broke up more giant corporations than Roosevelt. But some of his decisions outraged Roosevelt and other party leaders, especially on matters of the environment. Taft reluctantly agreed to seek reelection in 1912, but Roosevelt became his chief rival by forming the Progressive, or "Bull Moose," Party. Roosevelt drained off enough votes that the election went to Democrat Woodrow Wilson, and Taft gratefully retired. "I am glad to be going," he said. "This is the loneliest place in the world."

From 1913 to 1929, Taft enjoyed being a law professor at Yale, until President Harding enabled him to fulfill his lifelong dream by appointing him chief justice of the Supreme Court. Widely regarded as one of the most able chief justices ever, Taft served until 1930, when poor health forced him to resign. He died a few months later.

Paper Blossoms

In this project you can make paper blossoms that won't be quite as delicate as Japanese cherry blossoms, but they will make colorful decorations for your room or to brighten a gift package.

1 Place the 4 sheets of tissue paper on top of each other. Alternate colors: pink, white, pink, white. To fold the paper like a fan, fold in about ½ inch on the 5-inch side of the pile. Turn the sheets over and make a second ½-inch fold. Continue folding and turning all the way across, making a fan—or accordion—fold.

2 With scissors, round off all 4 corners.

3 Squeeze the center of the accordion fold and wrap a pipe cleaner around it. Wrap the end of the pipe cleaner around a second pipe cleaner to form a stem.

4 Lift the edges of each layer of paper and work them toward the center, creating a blossom shape. Make more blossoms. Depending on the purpose, try different colors.

Things You'll Need

4 sheets of thin paper for each blossom, 5 × 8 inches, in pink and white (tissue paper, wrapping paper, or origami paper all work well)

ruler

pencil

scissors

2 green pipe cleaners for each blossom (or white colored with green marking pen)

☆ ☆

A Baseball Leader

President Taft was an avid baseball fan and gave the game two of its great traditions. First, he introduced the practice of having a celebrity, such as the president, make the ceremonial first pitch of the season. Second, late in a game, Taft stood up to move around a little. To show respect for the president, other fans also stood up, launching the tradition of the seventh-inning stretch.

☆ ☆

From Clues to Quote

Fill in the answers to the clues. Transfer the letters to the numbered lines to reveal a statement made by President Taft. In honor of Taft's passion for baseball, all of the clues are related to the game. Some letters may be used more than once.

Clues	Words
1 The pitch was _____.	**1** __ __ __ __ 23 18 4 27
2 And the catcher _____ the ball.	**2** __ __ __ __ __ __ __ 27 25 5 13 13 7 27
3 The fielder made a great _____.	**3** __ __ __ __ __ 16 15 1 16 21
4 The _____ was way outside.	**4** __ __ __ __ __ 13 9 12 16 2
5 He ran outside the base _____.	**5** __ __ __ __ 26 18 6 22
6 The score for a solo home run is _____.	**6** __ __ __ 24 19 10
7 On a slow pitch you can _____ a base.	**7** __ __ __ __ __ 11 20 17 15 8
8 The pitch hit him below the ankle in the _____.	**8** __ __ __ __ 21 3 3 14

Famous Quote

" __ __ __   __ __ __ __ __ __ __ __ __   __ __ __ __ __
1 2 3   4 5 6 7 8 9 10 11 12   13 14 15 16 17

__ __   __ __ __   __ __ __ __ __ ."
18 19   20 21 22   23 24 25 26 27

Answers appear at the back of the book.

I don't even remember that I was ever president.

Woodrow Wilson

Twenty-eighth President, 1913–1921

Born *December 28, 1856, Staunton, Virginia*
Died *February 3, 1924, Washington, D.C.*

Woodrow Wilson lived two very different lives: he became an outstanding scholar, serving as a college professor and college president; then, in his mid-fifties, he entered politics as a governor before becoming president. As president, Wilson led the nation through World War I (1914–1918). He hoped that American influence could help create a lasting peace. Two of his most important ideas were an international organization to resolve conflicts (this became the League of Nations) and the concept of self-determination—that the people had the right to decide on their own government.

Born in Virginia, Wilson grew up in Georgia, where he struggled to overcome two serious handicaps. One problem was poor health, which kept him out of school until he was twelve years old. The other disability was being a slow learner. He didn't learn to read until age nine and always had trouble with math.

Wilson worked hard to improve in health and schooling. He graduated from Princeton in 1879 and entered law, hoping it would lead to a career in politics. He soon became bored with law, went back to college to earn a Ph.D. in political science, and became a college professor. He taught from 1885 to 1910 and was president of Princeton from 1902 to 1910.

In 1910, he was elected governor of New Jersey, even though he had no political experience. Wilson's writings and speeches about political reform appealed to voters, and they discovered that he had a warm and persuasive speaking style. After pushing through reforms in New Jersey, Wilson received the Democratic nomination for president in 1912.

Wilson served two terms as president. Important reforms became law during his presidency, including the amendment to the Constitution granting women the right to vote. The dominant issue involved World War I, which erupted in Europe in 1914. Wilson tried to remain neutral, and the Democrats' campaign slogan for his 1916 reelection campaign was "He kept us out of the war." Most Americans, however, sympathized with the Allied Powers (primarily England and France), and Germany's use of submarine warfare finally forced the president to ask Congress for a declaration of war.

Family Matters

President Wilson's first wife, Ellen, whom he had married in 1886, died in 1914. Although grief-stricken, the president fell in love a few months later with a widow, Edith Bolling Galt, and they were married in December 1915. They were not married in the White House, partly because two of the president's daughters had already been married in White House ceremonies: Jessie in 1913 and Eleanor in 1914.

Famous Phrases

President Wilson was a gifted speaker and also coined some phrases that were widely used. One was the "Great Melting Pot," referring to the nation as a mixing of people from different backgrounds. "A war to end all wars" and "Peace without victory" were others that became popular.

American troops and supplies tipped the balance in the war, and Germany was forced to surrender in November 1918. Wilson tried hard for a peace settlement based on his Fourteen Points, including a League of Nations to preserve the peace. But his plans were defeated in a bitter struggle with Senate Republicans. On a grueling speaking trip to build popular support, Wilson suffered a stroke that left him partially paralyzed.

Wilson was kept in seclusion by his wife until the final months of his presidency, by which time he was somewhat recovered. Although he felt he had failed as president, his belief in a world organization to keep peace was later revived and became the United Nations.

Summer Chicken Salad

Woodrow Wilson's favorite breakfast was grapefruit and raw eggs, which we don't recommend. But his favorite summertime meal was chicken salad. The following recipe is great anytime, especially for picnics, and can easily be expanded for large gatherings (the recipe suggests that, to serve 50, count on "1 gallon cooked chicken cubed").

1 Combine the chicken, celery, and almonds in a large bowl.

2 Stir in the mayonnaise, salt, and paprika.

3 Place one or two crisp lettuce leaves on each plate.

4 Place a portion of the salad on each of the dishes. Top with hard-cooked eggs, garnish with olives and pimientos, and serve.

Note: Since you're using mayonnaise, be sure to keep the salad chilled until it's ready to serve.

Remaking the Map of Europe

A major part of Wilson's Fourteen Points was the right of self-determination—the right of people who share a language and land area to have a government of their own choosing. The Allies' victory in World War I brought an end to three huge empires: the Ottoman Empire, the German Empire, and the Austro-Hungarian Empire. In creating new boundaries for Europe after the war, the Allied leaders followed the idea of self-determination as much as possible. Their work resulted in a very different map of Europe and the Middle East.

1 Look closely at the maps for 1914 and 1920. Make a list of the new countries and mandates that emerged. Mandates were territories assigned to one of the Great Powers by the League of Nations.

2 If you were planning a newspaper front page announcing the new map, what would you write as a headline? Try writing two or three subheadlines as well.

Answers appear at the back of the book.

War Measures

During the war, First Lady Edith Wilson kept twenty sheep grazing on the White House lawn. The goal was to save on the manpower of mowers, and the wool was donated to the Red Cross.

Things You'll Need

1 cup diced cooked chicken
½ cup chopped celery
¼ cup chopped almonds
½ cup mayonnaise
dash of salt
dash of paprika
4 hard-cooked eggs, sliced
½ cup sliced olives
½ cup chopped pimientos
lettuce
adult helper
measuring cup
cutting board
paring knife
large bowl
wooden spoon
4 serving dishes
MAKES 4 SERVINGS

Europe 1914

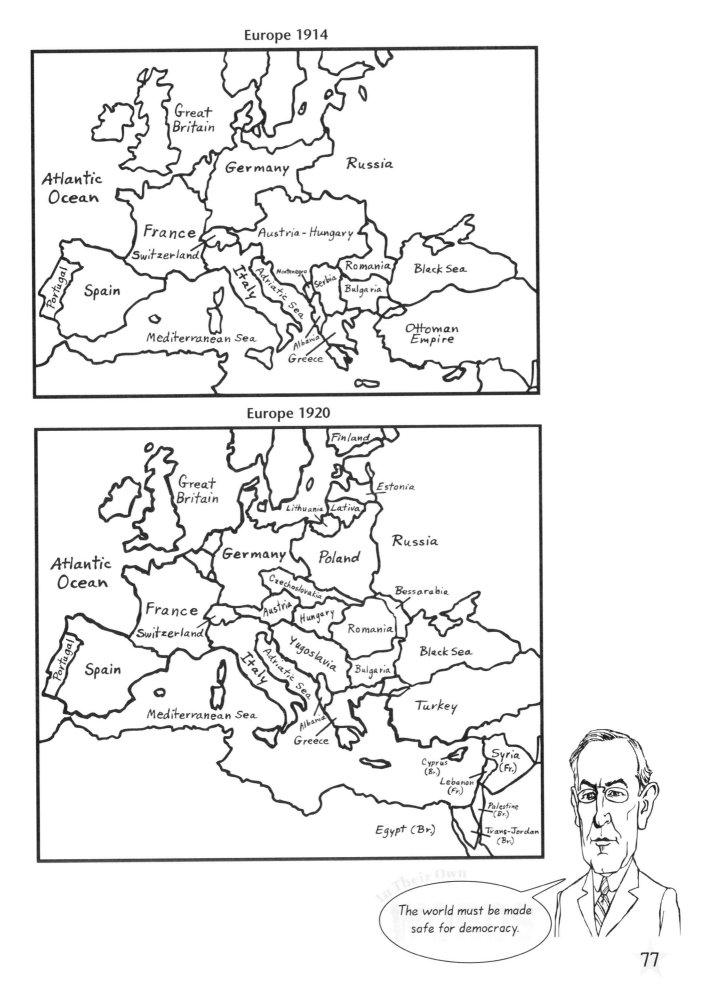

Europe 1920

The world must be made safe for democracy.

77

WARREN GAMALIEL HARDING

Twenty-ninth President, 1921–1923

Born *November 2, 1865, Corsica, Ohio*
Died *August 2, 1923, San Francisco, California*

☆☆☆☆☆☆☆☆☆☆☆

Family Matters

Many observers believed that Mrs. Florence Harding was the real power in the White House (although she could not control the crooked members of her husband's administration). She stuck by the president through all his difficulties and was with him when he died. Since the Hardings had no children, they made the most of their White House pets, including Laddie Boy, an Airedale. Laddie Boy was once host of his own White House birthday party, with several guests (neighborhood dogs). The cake was made of layers of dog biscuits topped with icing. A bronze statue of Laddie Boy is in the Smithsonian Institute.

☆☆☆☆☆☆☆☆☆☆☆

arren G. Harding was a tall, handsome man with a warm personality, an outgoing, friendly manner, and an appealing speaking voice. These qualities convinced many people that Harding "looked like a president." Unfortunately, few men have been less qualified by temperament or training for the nation's most demanding job. Historians generally agree that he was the least successful of our presidents.

Harding grew up in small-town Ohio and became a lifelong booster of the traditional small-town way of life. He became owner of the Marion *Star* newspaper and served as its editor for thirty-five years, until 1922.

Although he had little interest in politics at first, his wife, Florence, pressed him to become involved. He soon found that he enjoyed giving speeches and meeting people. He served in the Ohio senate for four years and then as lieutenant governor, from 1904 to 1905. After losing a race for governor, he was elected to the U.S. Senate and served from 1915 to 1921.

In 1920, the Republican Party leaders chose Harding as a compromise candidate largely because he was popular, looked presidential, and had no enemies. In the election, he promised war-weary voters a return to *normalcy*, a word he invented, and he won easily.

Harding disliked the pressures of the presidency from the first day, and he escaped from them whenever he could by playing golf or poker. He surrounded himself with so many of his old pals that they became known as the Ohio Gang or the Poker Cabinet. One of his most successful actions was to make Charles Evans Hughes his secretary of state. Hughes arranged the Washington Naval Conference, at which the major powers agreed to limit the size of their navies.

Others in Harding's cabinet became involved in bribery and corrupt practices. The most notorious case, called the Teapot Dome scandal, involved misuse of three oil reserves, which included one at Teapot Dome, Wyoming. As the first evidence of corruption emerged, Harding was devastated to find that his friends had betrayed him. He started a long railroad tour, hoping to restore the public's confidence in him. But he was already suffering from poor health and frazzled nerves. He became ill and died suddenly in a San Francisco hotel on August 2, 1923. Rumors that he had been poisoned were later discounted.

Headline Scramble

As a newspaper owner and editor for thirty-five years, Harding wrote his share of newspaper headlines. He could have had fun with this project using newspapers. It also makes a good traveling game.

1. Cut out 40 or 50 headlines from newspapers and magazines. Separate the words so that you have a pile of unconnected words.

2. To make the headline words easy to handle and store, copy or paste them on index cards, using a pen or computer. Cut up the cards so that the words remain separate. You can even back them with reusable adhesive so that the words stay in place on any solid surface.

3. Keep the words in a small box. Shake or stir the box to mix them. The box can also be handy when you travel; you can use the lid as a game board.

4. Now, try making your own crazy headlines. Take turns with a friend to see who makes the funniest combinations. Limit the length to six words.

Things You'll Need

scissors
several newspapers and news magazines
index cards
pen or computer
small box
2 sheets of reusable adhesive, available at craft stores (optional)

Word Detection

For each of the ten clues, write a five-letter word on the blank dashes. Spell the word with five of the six letters printed on that line. Place the sixth, or extra, letter in the far right column. Those letters also make a scrambled word. Unscramble them to find something associated with Harding.

1 The Republican _____   _ _ _ _ _ _   A P R P Y T   _

2 Open your mouth to   _ _ _ _ _ _   M K E P S A   _

3 Large presidential boat   _ _ _ _ _ _   C O Y A T H   _

4 Color of the executive mansion   _ _ _ _ _ _   H A T I W E   _

5 Choose by vote   _ _ _ _ _ _   T E D L C E   _

6 The Supreme _____   _ _ _ _ _ _   T R U E O C   _

7 A hunting dog   _ _ _ _ _ _   D N H U O T   _

8 Harding's favorite game   _ _ _ _ _ _   K P R T O E   _

9 Washington Naval Conference involved _____   _ _ _ _ _ _   H P O I S S   _

10 Harding traveled by _____   _ _ _ _ _ _   T A E I R N   _

Answers appear at the back of the book.

Harding's Words

In addition to *normalcy*, Harding is credited with coining the phrase *our founding fathers* to refer to the founders of the nation. He also invented a word, *bloviating*, to describe the practice of speaking many words without really saying anything. Many people said that the word was a good description of Harding's speeches.

Front Porch Campaigner

Like President McKinley in 1896, Harding decided to run his presidential campaign from the front porch of his Ohio home. After the election, the porch had to be rebuilt because of the wear and tear from supporters and journalists.

America wants a return to normalcy.

Calvin Coolidge

Thirtieth President, 1923–1929

Born *July 4, 1872, Plymouth, Vermont*
Died *November 5, 1933, Northampton, Massachusetts*

Calvin Coolidge could not have chosen a better time to become president. After the horror of World War I (1914–1918) and postwar economic blues, the United States was entering one of its greatest periods of growth and prosperity. These were the fast-paced years that became known as the Roaring Twenties or the Jazz Age, and the president did not have to do much to help Americans enjoy the good times. Calvin Coolidge turned out to be the perfect man for the times.

He was born in Vermont and was a New Englander through and through. He believed in working hard and saving money. Although he liked conversation with close friends, he spoke so little that he became known as Silent Cal. "If you don't say anything," he explained, "no one can call on you to repeat it."

After college and law school, he went into politics, spending the first thirty years of his career in Massachusetts. Beginning as a city councilman in 1899, he moved to the state legislature in 1907, then became lieutenant governor from 1916 to 1918 and governor from 1919 to 1923. His firm stand during a police strike gave him nationwide popularity with voters. "There is no right to strike against the public safety," he declared, "by anybody, anywhere, anytime." He was rewarded with the vice presidency in 1920, and in 1924, after succeeding Harding, he won an overwhelming victory for another four years as president.

Coolidge remained popular throughout his presidency, especially with businesspeople. He did little to interfere with the fast-growing economy. In fact, he vetoed legislation designed to help those who were not sharing in the prosperity, such as farm families who could not make their mortgage payments. While he was a thorough worker, he did manage to sleep a lot—nine hours a night plus a two-hour afternoon nap.

As the prosperity continued through the decade, it seems likely Coolidge could have been reelected in 1928. However, with his usual economy of words, he said, "I do not choose to run for president." The public did not know that he had suffered a heart attack, and he feared that the strain of the presidency might be too much. Timing favored Coolidge again: he left office months before the stock market crash that ushered in the Great Depression. He retired to his Northampton, Massachusetts, home, where he lived until his death in 1933.

Family Matters

The Coolidges generally enjoyed life in the White House. First Lady Grace Coolidge was the opposite of her husband. She was warm, outgoing, and talkative. Reporters nicknamed her Sunny.

The Coolidges had two sons and quite a menagerie: twelve dogs, two cats, canaries, a thrush, a donkey named Ebenezer, a wallaby, a lion cub, and Enoch, a white goose.

President on Horseback

President Coolidge enjoyed horseback riding, but he became fond of mechanical horses and had one installed in the White House. Powered by electricity, the horse could give a rough ride, even bucking like a bronco, which the president seemed to enjoy.

If You're Not Busy, Dad

Coolidge was the only president to be sworn in by his father. The senior Coolidge was a justice of the peace in Plymouth Notch, Vermont, where Vice President Coolidge was vacationing when the news came of Harding's death.

Maple Syrup Muffins

In his autobiography, which he wrote after he retired, Coolidge said that his favorite chore on the family's Vermont farm was tapping the maple trees, then boiling the sap for hours until it became syrup. Here is an old New England recipe for making maple syrup muffins. Be sure to use pure maple syrup, not artificial.

1 Have an adult preheat the oven to 375 degrees F.

2 In a large bowl, combine the flour, baking powder, and salt.

3 Break the egg into the second bowl and beat it. Add the maple syrup, milk, cooking oil, and orange zest. Mix well.

4 Make a large indentation in the center of the dry ingredients. Pour the liquid ingredients into the hole and stir with a wooden spoon. Stir just enough to combine. The batter will be lumpy, but don't overmix.

5 Pour the batter into the muffin tins lined with muffin papers so that each muffin is about two-thirds full. Bake at 375 degrees F for 18 to 20 minutes.

6 Have an adult use oven mitts to take the muffins out of the oven and put them on a cooling rack. Allow the muffins to cool before serving.

Things You'll Need

1½ cups all-purpose flour
2 teaspoons baking powder
½ teaspoon salt
1 egg
½ cup pure maple syrup
½ cup milk
¼ cup vegetable cooking oil
½ teaspoon grated orange zest
adult helper
measuring cup
measuring spoon
2 large bowls
wooden spoon
egg beater
2 muffin tins
muffin papers
oven mitts
cooling rack
MAKES 12 MUFFINS

Plains Indian Headdress

In 1927, President Coolidge was made an honorary member of the Sioux Nation, with the tribal name of Chief Leading Eagle. During summers in the Black Hills of South Dakota, the president liked to walk around in his Sioux finery, which included a headdress made with eagle feathers. The eagle feathers were awarded for special feats. Great chiefs had headdresses that stretched down their backs almost to the ground. Here's a way to make a simple headdress of your own.

1 Measure a strip of tagboard about 3 inches wide and long enough to reach around your head plus 2 inches. Cut out the strip. Use crayons or a black pen to decorate it with traditional Native American patterns such as zigzag lines or triangles. Fit it around your head so that it's comfortable. Overlap the ends and staple it.

2 On a sheet of white paper, draw a feather shape to use as a pattern. The feather should be 6 to 8 inches long and about 2½ or 3 inches wide. Draw a black line down the center and color the tip of the feather dark brown.

3 Cut out the feather and use it as a pattern to make 10 or 11 more.

4 Glue the feathers around the headband. Glue a piece of a cotton ball at the base of each feather so it looks like the fluffy feathers used on real headdresses.

Things You'll Need

strip of tagboard, about 3 inches wide
ruler
pencil
scissors
crayons
black pen
stapler
several sheets of white paper
white glue
cotton balls

The business of America is business.

HERBERT HOOVER

Thirty-first President, 1929–1933

Born *August 10, 1874, West Branch, Iowa*
Died *October 20, 1964, New York, New York*

Family Matters

Hoover married Lou Henry in 1899, and the couple went immediately to China, where he served as the country's mining engineer for a time. Mrs. Hoover, who had an ear for languages, became quite fluent in Chinese. Years later, in the White House, the two sometimes spoke in Chinese to preserve their privacy. The Hoovers had two sons, Herbert and Allen.

☆ ☆ ☆ ☆ ☆ ☆ ☆ ☆ ☆ ☆

Namesakes

Hooverville wasn't the only thing to be named after Herbert Hoover. Hoover Dam, on the Colorado River near Las Vegas, is one of the largest hydroelectric dams in the nation. It was built in 1936, but it was not named for the former president until 1947.

An Austrian astronomer who discovered an asteroid in 1920 named it *Hooveria* to honor Hoover for his World War I relief efforts.

☆ ☆ ☆ ☆ ☆ ☆ ☆ ☆ ☆ ☆

Following nearly a decade of prosperity under Republican presidents—from 1920 to 1928—voters eagerly elected another Republican, Herbert Hoover, in 1928. Unfortunately, only a few months after Hoover took office, the stock market crashed and the American economy slid into the Great Depression. Many Americans for the first time in history faced terrible poverty and looked to the government for help. When President Hoover offered no plan for recovery or for emergency aid, many people thought he was heartless and uncaring. Nothing could have been farther from the truth. Herbert Hoover had spent much of his life, and his wealth, helping people in need. What went wrong when he was president?

Herbert Hoover was born in Iowa, grew up in Oregon, and attended college at Stanford in California. He became a mining engineer and developed a special knack for finding rich deposits of gold, silver, zinc, and oil. He worked in Australia, China, and Africa. By his mid-thirties, he had become wealthy and was considered one of the world's leading authorities on mining.

During World War I (1914–1918), Hoover became the major organizer of emergency relief for starving refugees in Belgium and other European countries, often using his own money. When the United States entered the war in 1917, he served as U.S. food administrator, devising creative ways for Americans to save food for the war effort. After the war, he spent five more years in European relief efforts, then served in the Harding and Coolidge cabinets as secretary of commerce (1921–1928) before being elected president.

As the nation sank into the depths of the Depression, Hoover told people that "prosperity is just around the corner." He thought that the economy would soon improve, as it had in the past, and trusted that private and community charities could relieve the suffering until things got better. He also felt that government aid would make people dependent on the government. When war veterans marched into Washington hoping to receive service bonuses before the official date of 1945, Hoover refused to consider their demands. The veterans built a village of shacks on government land, calling the area Hooverville. The president had the army move in, force the men out, and level the shanties. It was a sad episode for a man who cared so deeply about helping others.

After losing the 1932 election to Democrat Franklin D. Roosevelt, Hoover remained active in public affairs for another thirty years. During and after World War II (1939–1945), he again headed relief efforts in Europe. He also chaired two projects, called the Hoover Commission, which made important recommendations on streamlining the executive branch of the government. He died in 1964 at the age of ninety.

Overconfidence?

Hoover had great confidence in the idea that the American economy had reached so close to perfection that poverty and hunger would soon disappear. "We in America today," he said, "are nearer to the final triumph over poverty than ever before in the history of any land. The poorhouse is vanishing from among us." This strong belief made it difficult for him to consider government programs to end the Depression.

Colorful Crystals from Coal

In his mining ventures, Herbert Hoover became an expert on many kinds of minerals and rocks. His book, *Principles of Mining*, published in 1908, remained a classic text for engineering students for more than fifty years. This project invites you to have some fun with crystals made from coal.

1. Measure 2 tablespoons each of liquid blueing, laundry detergent, salt, and ammonia into a small jar. Have an adult helper supervise this mixing. Avoid breathing the ammonia fumes as much as possible. Stir with an old tablespoon or plastic picnic spoon.

2. Place 3 or 4 charcoal briquettes on a disposable pie tin. Add a few drops of food coloring on each briquette.

3. Pour some of the detergent, salt, and ammonia solution over the top of the charcoal pieces. While the crystals are forming, replenish your supply of solution.

4. As you enjoy the beautiful colors and shapes that emerge, repeat the process with 3 or 4 more briquettes.

Things You'll Need

adult helper
measuring spoon
liquid blue laundry detergent
iodized salt (table salt)
small bottle of ammonia
small jar
plastic picnic spoon or old table spoon
8 to 10 charcoal briquettes
disposable pie tin
food coloring—any colors

Printing with Junk

During the Great Depression, people found many uses for junk—anything that others had discarded. People even moved into city dumps and built shacks out of discarded items. Artists who could not afford to buy supplies also began to use junk in creative ways. In this project you can use small junk items to print an abstract design or collage.

1 Spread several sheets of newspaper over your work surface. Place a sheet of paper or newsprint on top. To print, simply press a small item into an ink pad and then onto the newsprint.

2 Place printed items at different angles to make interesting patterns. Place them close together and even overlapping.

3 Continue printing until you have pretty well covered a sheet with an abstract design.

4 Print more collages with different objects. Choose the artwork you like best to hang on the wall of your room.

Things You'll Need

small sheets of newspaper
large sheets of newsprint or other inexpensive paper
collection of "junk" (found objects), such as corks, small lids or bottle caps, coins, bolts, nuts, parts of toys or machines or tools, film canisters, and anything else you can find
ink pads—2 or 3 colors

I have no fears for the future of our country. It is bright with hope.

83

FRANKLIN DELANO
ROOSEVELT

★ ★

Thirty-second President, 1933–1945

Born *January 30, 1882, Hyde Park, New York*
Died *April 12, 1945, Warm Springs, Georgia*

hen Franklin Delano Roosevelt was elected president in 1932, people did not know what to expect. Some wondered if a man crippled by polio could handle the strains of the presidency. And others wondered how a man from a wealthy family could understand the hardships of the Great Depression. Roosevelt surprised everyone, even his critics. For the next twelve years, until his sudden death in 1945, Roosevelt led the nation through two of its greatest crises: the Depression and World War II. He proved to be a leader of great confidence, in himself and in the American people.

Roosevelt was an inexperienced member of the New York State Senate when President Wilson chose him, on the basis of family connections, to be assistant secretary of the navy in 1913. But after an unsuccessful campaign for vice president in 1920, Roosevelt's political career seemed over when he was stricken with polio at the age of thirty-eight. His wife, Eleanor, helped convince him that even though he would never have the use of his legs, he could return to political life. Over the next few years, he managed to turn the tragic illness into personal strength, gaining a new confidence in himself along with compassion for the suffering of others. He was elected governor of New York in 1928 and reelected in 1930, before winning the presidency.

First Dog

Roosevelt's pet Scotty, named Fala, was the president's constant companion. The White House press corps called Fala the Informer because they knew that wherever the dog was, the president was not far away.

☆ ☆

Family Matters

Franklin married a distant cousin, Eleanor Roosevelt, in 1905. They had six children, although one died in infancy. Eleanor Roosevelt played a more active role in government than any other presidential wife. She served in the National Youth Administration and the Office of Civilian Defense during the war. The president relied on her as his "eyes, ears, and legs" because she traveled throughout the country and reported to him on people's responses to various programs. Mrs. Roosevelt also wrote a daily newspaper column called "My Day" as well as several books. After her husband's death, she represented the United States in the United Nations. Both Eleanor and Franklin were also cousins of President Theodore Roosevelt.

☆ ☆

During Roosevelt's first three months in office, his promised New Deal for all Americans began to take shape. Rather than a blueprint, the New Deal turned out to be a series of experiments to help lift the nation out of the Depression. Some programs were designed to solve problems that had led to the Depression, such as weaknesses in the banking system. Other measures put the unemployed to work on public works projects, such as building roads, parks, and dams. Although the New Deal did not end the Depression, it helped Americans regain hope.

Roosevelt was easily elected to a second term in 1936 and in 1940 became the first president elected to a third term, as the shadow of war loomed over the nation. The demands of World War II (1939–1945) helped improve the U.S. economy. By working closely with the nation's allies, especially Great Britain, Roosevelt helped forge the victory over military dictatorships in Germany, Italy, and Japan. His inspired wartime leadership included promoting what he called the Four Freedoms (freedom of speech, of worship, from want, and from fear) and the creation of the United Nations.

Although FDR was elected to a fourth term in 1944, his health was already failing. He died in April 1945, when victory in the war was finally in sight.

Feminine Firsts

In 1933, Roosevelt appointed Frances Perkins to be secretary of labor, the first woman to hold a cabinet post. She remained in the office until 1945 and played an important part in New Deal legislation, most notably the Social Security Act, which provided retirement and other benefits to millions of Americans.

The president was also the first to appoint African Americans to important government positions, with Mary McLeod Bethune in the National Youth Administration being the first.

Victory Garden Planter

During the war, the Roosevelt administration encouraged Americans to grow victory gardens. By growing vegetables and fruits for their own consumption, people made more food available for men and women in uniform and for aid to allied countries. The victory gardens were a great success, as millions of people participated, producing 40 percent of the table vegetables consumed in 1944 alone. This project offers a good way to start seedlings for a garden—and it's fun.

1 Place the shell halves in empty egg cartons. Fill each shell with a few spoonfuls of potting soil.

2 Place 4 or 6 seeds in each shell, pushing them almost to the bottom of the shell. The seed varieties listed here are good choices because they grow quite fast.

3 Place your planter in a bright location, but it shouldn't get more than 1 or 2 hours of direct sun each day. Keep the soil moist.

4 When the seedlings are close to 2 inches high, thin them by pulling out all but the best 2 or 3. Discard the others.

5 When the seedlings have grown to a height of 4 or 5 inches, transplant them into a garden or window box.

Things You'll Need

shells from about a dozen eggs—in halves and rinsed clean

2 egg cartons

gardening trowel or old spoon

potting soil

seeds for green beans, carrots, snap peas, radishes

tap water

Build a Word

Figure out the clue for each of the seven words and write your answers in the spaces. All of the words have something to do with Franklin Roosevelt and his presidency. The letters in the squares will form an eighth item, but it's scrambled and it's two words. Unscramble it to find another connection to FDR.

1 Economic hard times were known as the _____.

1 ▢ _ _ _ _ _ _ _ _ _

2 Polio meant Roosevelt lost the use of his _____.

2 _ ▢ _ _

3 FDR's middle name

3 _ _ _ _ ▢ _

4 Roosevelt was assistant secretary of the _____.

4 _ ▢ _ _

5 Roosevelt was president during the Second World _____.

5 ▢ _ _

6 Roosevelt served in the New York State _____.

6 _ _ _ _ _ ▢

7 FDR never lost a presidential _____.

7 _ ▢ _ _ _ _ _

8 _ _ _   _ _ _ _

Answers appear at the back of the book.

Harry S Truman

Thirty-third President, 1945–1953

Born May 8, 1884, Lamar, Missouri
Died December 26, 1972, Kansas City, Missouri

Perhaps no other president has had to make as many crucial decisions as Harry S Truman, and all of them had to be made under severe time pressure. It was Truman who had to make the fateful decision about using the first atomic bomb. And he was the president who had to confront the aggression of the Soviet Union and other Communist powers after World War II. Although he was often severely criticized at the time, history has supported almost every urgent decision he made.

There was not a lot in Truman's early life to suggest his future strengths and skills. He grew up in small-town Missouri, working the family farm and doing odd jobs. After performing well as an artillery commander in World War I (1914–1918), he tried opening a haberdashery (men's clothing store), but the business failed within two years. He served in county offices until being elected to the U.S. Senate in 1934 and reelected in 1940. Truman gained considerable fame by exposing fraud by companies supplying the military, and Roosevelt had him put on the 1944 ticket as vice president.

Truman did not know until after Roosevelt's death in April 1945 that the United States had been developing an atomic bomb, hoping to achieve that goal before Nazi Germany did. It was up to Truman to decide if this terrifying weapon should be used as a way to end World War II. Although Germany was already out of the war, it was believed that the Allies would have to invade Japan, an event that could cost up to one million American lives. Truman ordered the first atomic bomb dropped on Hiroshima on August 6, and when Japan still did not surrender, the second on Nagasaki three days later. Japan then surrendered, and the war was over.

Although World War II was over, Americans were shocked to discover that they faced a new menace as Soviet Communism swept over Eastern Europe. Truman acted quickly and decisively: first, by establishing the Truman Doctrine, providing aid to Greece and Turkey to combat Communism; second, by developing the Marshall Plan, granting huge amounts of aid to rebuild Europe; and third, by forming the North Atlantic Treaty Organization (NATO), a defensive military alliance. In Asia, when Communist North Korea invaded South Korea in June 1950, Truman received United Nations approval to send in troops. This "police action" was the Korean War.

☆☆☆☆☆☆☆☆☆☆

What Does the S Stand For?

When Harry Truman was born, the family disagreed over whether his middle name should be Shippe or Solomon—the names of his grandfathers. Truman's solution was to use only the S rather than upset either branch of the family. Because it's not an abbreviation for either name, you don't have to put a period after the S.

☆☆☆☆☆☆☆☆☆☆

In spite of his courageous actions, few people thought Truman could be elected in 1948, running against Republican Thomas E. Dewey. But Truman surprised everyone. He launched a "whistle-stop" railroad campaign, crisscrossing the nation, delivering three hundred fifty speeches as people cheered, "Give 'em Hell, Harry!" He won the election, despite the *Chicago Tribune* famously running a headline blaring "Dewey Defeats Truman." Over the next four years, however, his Fair Deal agenda promoting civil rights ran into stiff opposition in Congress.

Truman retired rather than seeking reelection in 1952. He wrote three autobiographical works during his long retirement. He died in 1972.

The Peace Eagle

Things You'll Need

Styrofoam cup and lid
pencil
Styrofoam take-out tray or grocery-store tray
scissors
scrap paper
ballpoint pen
white glue
stamp pad (or tempera paint or poster paint)
paper or envelopes

President Truman was troubled by the symbol of the eagle on the presidential seal. Until his term, the eagle had been looking toward the talon holding the arrows of war. Truman had the seal redesigned so that the head is now looking toward the talon holding the olive branches of peace. In this project, you'll make your own stamp seal, either a model of the presidential seal or a stamp of your own design.

1 Use the top of the cup (not the lid) to draw a circle on the tray. Cut out the circle.

2 Use scrap paper and pencil to draw the symbol you want on your stamp. Copy it in ballpoint pen on the Styrofoam circle. (Press hard so that the symbol is indented in the Styrofoam.)

3 Put the lid on the cup and glue the circle to the lid. The cup, turned upside down, becomes the stamp.

4 Coat the design with ink from the stamp pad. (You can also use tempera or poster paint.) Press the inked design onto paper, like a letterhead, or onto envelopes.

Family Matters

Truman called First Lady Elizabeth "Bess" Truman the Boss, and daughter Margaret the Boss's Boss or My Baby. The White House staff labeled them The Three Musketeers because they enjoyed each other's company so much.

The president was a talented pianist and sometimes accompanied Margaret's singing. Her attempt to launch a singing career was not successful; she did much better as a writer of mystery novels.

Breaking Secret Codes

The Truman administration formed the Central Intelligence Agency (CIA) in 1947. One of the CIA's jobs was to decipher secret messages sent by Communist agents. CIA code specialists learned to break simple codes first, like this one called the Julius Caesar cipher. (It was named after the Roman conqueror because he used it.)

In this code, two alphabets are used. The second alphabet is shifted a secret number of letters underneath the first alphabet. In this example, the secret number is 7. The second alphabet is shifted seven letters to the right. To write the letter A, for instance, you move seven letters to H, and you would start your second alphabet there, as shown.

(1) A B C D E F G H I J K L M N O P Q R S T U V W X Y Z

(2) T U V W X Y Z A B C D E F G H I J K L M N O P Q R S

In this shift code, the word THE would be MAX.

Try exchanging short secret messages with a friend. For a real challenge, switch to another secret number (under 10). Write a message in the new code, and see if others can decipher it.

Presidential Mottoes

President Truman had small signs on his desk containing his favorite mottoes. One read simply, "The buck stops here." Another contained a quote by author Mark Twain: "Always do right. This will gratify some people and astonish the rest." And a late addition offered, "If you can't stand the heat, get out of the kitchen."

Within the first few months, I discovered that being President is like riding a tiger. A man has to keep on riding or be swallowed.

DWIGHT DAVID EISENHOWER

Thirty-fourth President, 1953–1961

Born October 14, 1890, Denison, Texas
Died March 28, 1969, Washington, D.C.

eneral Dwight David Eisenhower was far from being a career politician. Until he ran for president in 1952, no one even knew what political party he belonged to. It didn't really matter, though. Everyone just wanted to know if he would run for president. As supreme Allied commander in Europe, General Eisenhower had led the Allied forces to victory over Nazi Germany in World War II (1939–1945). Ike, as he was known to a grateful public, announced that he was a Republican, and he defeated Democrat Adlai Stevenson in 1952 and again in 1956.

Eisenhower was a genial but reserved man with a famous grin. His mild manner belied the fact that as a boy growing up in poverty in Abilene, Texas, he and his five brothers had been known as scrappy fighters. They needed to be because of the teasing they took for wearing hand-me-downs, including their mother's worn-out shoes.

Throughout his school years, Dwight was a so-so student, including his years at West Point, 1911 to 1915. He was bored with school but stuck with it to play football. A knee injury ended his football career, but he completed his education. A decade later, he began to hit his stride at the Command and General Staff School, 1925 to 1926, finishing first in a class of 275.

He served in the Philippines from 1935 to 1939 and was made commander of the Allied forces landing in North Africa in 1942 during World War II. Eisenhower played a major role in planning D-Day, the invasion of Normandy (France) June 6, 1944, a giant step in the Allies' liberation of Europe from the grip of Nazi Germany. After the war, he served as chief of staff (1945–1948) and then became president of Columbia University (1948–1953), except for a leave of absence in 1950 to take command of NATO (North Atlantic Treaty Organization) forces in Europe.

As president, Eisenhower reorganized the country's defenses and worked to speed a compromise truce in the Korean War. Although not eager to push for civil rights, he did send troops into Little Rock, Arkansas, in September 1957, to ensure that the city's high school would enroll its first African American students.

Considering the social and political turmoil of the 1960s, the Eisenhower years in the 1950s came to feel like a period of calm. People had the impression that the president spent a good deal of time practicing his

So Much for Yearbook Prediction

When Eisenhower graduated from Abilene High School in 1909, the yearbook predicted that he would become a history professor and his brother, Edgar, would become president of the United States.

putting on a White House green that had been installed for him next to the Rose Garden. The country's prosperity and Ike's enormous popularity led many people to overlook his lack of vigorous action on issues such as civil rights, organized crime, and decaying cities. His campaign slogan, "I like Ike," summed up the mood of the country. After leaving the White House, Eisenhower lived quietly on his farm outside Gettysburg, Pennsylvania, until his death in 1969.

☆ ☆

Family Matters

When Eisenhower married nineteen-year-old Marie "Mamie" Doud in 1916, she had to adjust to life on his meager army pay after growing up in an affluent family. She put up with cramped living quarters and dinners at a Mexican restaurant where a meal for two cost $1.25, including the tip. She was also cheerful about having to move almost thirty times in the next thirty-five years. Mamie and Dwight had two sons, but one died of scarlet fever as a child. In 1980, a year after Mamie's death, her birthplace in Boone, Iowa, was made a historic site. Abigail Adams, wife of John Adams, is the only other first lady to have been so honored.

☆ ☆

Ways to Say Thanks

America and its allies heaped awards on the general for his wartime leadership. Some examples: Scotland gave him the lifetime use of Culzean Castle; from Denmark came the Order of the Elephant; the Grand Cross of the Legion of Honor was awarded by France; and Ethiopia awarded him the Order of Solomon with Placque and Cordon. Eisenhower also won numerous awards in the United States, including the Distinguished Service Medal and the Oak Leaf Cluster.

Prune or Apricot Whip

President Eisenhower was an enthusiastic cook who even took to grilling on the White House roof. He was well known for his vegetable soup, charcoal-broiled steaks, potato salad, cornmeal pancakes, and his favorite dessert: prune or apricot whip.

1 Have an adult preheat the oven to 300 degrees F.

2 Place the cooked or canned prunes or apricots in a large strainer. Use the back of a spoon to work the fruit through the strainer into a measuring cup. Continue until the fruit measures ¾ cup. Add a little sugar and stir.

3 Spoon the fruit into a saucepan. Cook the fruit over low to medium heat until it's as thick as jam or marmalade about 10 minutes. Stir frequently with a wooden spoon.

4 Stir in the lemon juice and salt. Turn off the heat and let the mixture cool.

5 Beat the egg whites in a large bowl until stiff. Carefully fold the fruit into the egg whites.

6 Fill a large pan one-quarter full of hot water.

7 Spoon the mixture into a straight-sided baking dish. Set the baking dish in the pan of hot water. Bake at 300 degrees F until the dessert is firm when you press it lightly with your finger (about 45 minutes).

8 Have an adult use oven mitts to remove the dish from the oven.

9 Allow the prune or apricot whip to cool for a few minutes. Serve with whipped cream.

Things You'll Need

cooked or canned prunes or apricots
sugar to taste (start with 1 teaspoon)
1 tablespoon lemon juice
⅛ teaspoon salt
3 egg whites
tap water
whipped cream
adult helper
measuring cup
measuring spoon
strainer
wooden spoon
1- or 2-quart saucepan
large bowl
egg beater
large pan
straight-sided baking dish
oven mitts
MAKES 4 SERVINGS

Yut-Nori: A Korean Board Game

During the presidential campaign of 1952, General Eisenhower promised that if elected, he would go to Korea to try to end the war. After the election, he did go to Korea. Even though the journey did not directly lead to peace, it showed the nation and the world that the new president was determined to achieve an end to the bitter conflict. (A truce was signed several months later.) To commemorate Ike's journey, you can construct a popular Korean board game called *Yut-Nori*. Korean children often play it between the lunar New Year and the first full moon.

Things You'll Need

2, 3, or 4 players
drawing compass or plate, about 12 inches in diameter
pencil
tagboard, about 12–14 inches square
scissors
48 sticker dots—4 different colors (12 of each)
sticker star
2 to 4 miniature toys to use as game pieces
4 craft sticks
Magic Markers—2 or 3 colors

1 Use a drawing compass or a large plate to draw a 12-inch-diameter circle on the poster board or tag board. Cut out the circle.

2 Arrange sticker dots around the outside edge of the game board. Use 4 different colors, alternating colors and placing them about ¼ inch apart.

3 Place the sticker star over one of the dots. This will be both the Start and Finish for the game.

4 Have one miniature toy as a game piece for each player.

5 Decorate *one* side of each of the 4 craft sticks with Magic Markers. Use geometric designs or the sun, moon, and stars in any colors you choose.

6 Each player takes a turn by tossing the sticks in the air, then moves his or her game piece according to how the sticks have landed:

- if all 4 decorated sides are up, move 4 dots clockwise from the star;
- 3 sticks with decorations up, move 3 dots;
- 2 decorated sticks, move 2 dots;
- 1 decorated stick, move 1 dot;
- if all sticks land blank side up, go back 4 dots.

7 If a player lands on a dot that's occupied, he or she has to go back to Start and toss again.

8 The first player to go all the way around the board is the winner.

The United States never lost a soldier or a foot of ground during my administration. We kept the peace.

JOHN FITZGERALD KENNEDY

Thirty-fifth President, 1961–1963

Born *May 29, 1917, Brookline, Massachusetts*
Died *November 22, 1963, Dallas, Texas*

Even before he became the youngest man elected president, John F. Kennedy seemed to have everything a person could want. He was handsome, a good athlete, wealthy, a war hero, successful as both a writer and a politician, and from 1953 on, married to a beautiful socialite, Jacqueline Lee Bouvier Kennedy. But Kennedy's life was not as perfect as it seemed. He suffered from chronic back pain and survived two nearly fatal illnesses. Historian Arthur M. Schlesinger, who was an adviser to President Kennedy, may have described his life best as "the triumph, hard-bought and well-earned, of a gallant and collected human being over the anguish of life."

Kennedy was the second of nine children in the family of Joseph and Rose Fitzgerald Kennedy, a wealthy and well-known Massachusetts family. He was educated at Harvard. While working for his father, who was ambassador to Great Britain, he wrote a thesis that in 1940 became a highly regarded book, *Why England Slept,* on England's failure to stand up to German dictator Adolf Hitler on the eve of World War II (1939–1945).

During the war, Kennedy served as the commander of a PT boat in the South Pacific. The boat was cut in two by a Japanese warship in 1943, killing two of his crewmen. Kennedy reinjured his back but was still able to swim for four hours, towing a wounded crewman by holding the strap of the man's life jacket in his teeth. The incident was the subject for a book and a movie titled *PT 109.*

After the war and a brief stint as a journalist, Kennedy went into politics and quickly proved to be a skilled campaigner. He served in the House of Representatives from 1947 to 1953, then was elected to the Senate in 1952 and reelected in 1958. In 1960, Kennedy was elected president, winning by a narrow margin over Republican Richard M. Nixon.

As president, Kennedy became increasingly popular, partly because of his ability to communicate with people and partly because of his honesty. He started the Peace Corps and other programs such as the Alliance for Progress that showed a new commitment to helping less developed countries. And when he made mistakes, he was willing to admit them and move on.

Family Matters

First Lady Jacqueline Kennedy was one of the most popular presidential wives and also the most glamorous. Her clothing styles were quickly imitated by women throughout the country and the world. Jackie oversaw a major restoration of White House furnishings. She then led a televised tour of the changes in 1962, charming the viewing public and surprising many with her knowledge of history.

Jackie and John had two children, Caroline and John Jr., and Jackie worked hard to make the White House a comfortable family home as well as a national treasure.

JFK Firsts

Kennedy was the first Catholic to be elected president. He was also the first to be born in the twentieth century, as well as the first to appoint a family member to the cabinet, when brother Robert became attorney general. In addition, he was the first president to win a Pulitzer Prize (for *Profiles of Courage*, which he wrote while recovering from back surgery in 1955) and the first to serve in the navy.

A Dangerous Target

Kennedy survived a long list of childhood illnesses, including scarlet fever, appendicitis, bronchitis, chicken pox, measles, whooping cough, and tonsillitis. He was sick so often that his brothers joked that a mosquito took a great risk in biting him.

In October 1962, Kennedy stood up to Soviet Premier Nikita Khrushchev in a showdown that became known as the Cuban Missile Crisis. Kennedy went on television to give the American people a step-by-step explanation of the event. The Soviets had boldly tried to set up missile sites in Cuba, only 90 miles from the U.S. coast. Kennedy ordered warships to block the Soviet ships, and Khrushchev finally backed down and ordered the ships to turn around. Kennedy also took a strong stand on civil rights as African Americans and other minorities struggled to overcome racial discrimination and prejudice. "This nation," he declared, "for all its hopes and boasts, will not be fully free until all its citizens are free."

In November 1963, on a political trip to Dallas, Texas, with his wife, Jacqueline, the president was shot and fatally wounded by a lone gunman, Lee Harvey Oswald.

JFK Letter Puzzle

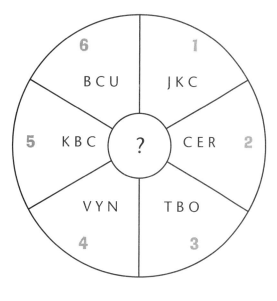

In this puzzle, you have to figure out what the missing letter is. The letter is always the same. That letter will fit with the groups of three letters to form six 4-letter words relating to Kennedy.

1 People often called Kennedy _____.

2 Kennedy's administration helped _____ relations.

3 Kennedy was commander of his _____.

4 Before he was president, he was in the _____.

5 Kennedy suffered from _____ pain.

6 _____ was invaded during his administration.

Answers appear at the back of the book.

Cape Cod Fish Chowder

President Kennedy had a number of favorite foods, including tomato soup topped with whipped cream. But the greatest favorite of all was fish chowder, and you can try this modified version of the traditional Cape Cod recipe. One way we've modified it is to substitute clam broth for the fish stock, which was made by cooking the fish skeleton and head to make a broth.

1 With an adult's help, place the bacon in a small skillet and cook it over low heat until well done. Drain onto paper towels. Break the bacon into small pieces and set aside. Pour the drippings into the saucepan.

2 Heat the bacon drippings, add the onion, and cook over low heat until golden brown. Add the potatoes and stir until well coated. Add the clam broth.

3 Cut the fish into chunks and add it to the pot. Partially cover the pot and simmer for about 15 minutes, or until the potatoes are tender and the fish is cooked through.

4 Stir in the cream, half-and-half, or milk. Heat slowly without boiling. Add the bacon pieces.

5 Just before serving, add the butter. Salt and pepper to taste. When the butter has melted, stir and serve.

Connecticut version: New Englanders argue a lot about the best chowder. Some Cape Cod cooks insist on what is called Connecticut fish chowder: Instead of cream or milk, use 1 cup canned tomatoes (undrained) plus 1/2 teaspoon dried marjoram or thyme.

Things You'll Need

2 slices of bacon

1 onion, peeled and diced

2 medium-size potatoes, peeled and diced

2 cups clam broth

1 pound fillet of cod, haddock, scrod, or other firm white fish

1 cup cream, half-and-half, or milk

1 tablespoon butter

salt

freshly ground pepper

adult helper

measuring cup

measuring spoon

paring knife

cutting board

small skillet

paper towels

2-quart saucepan with lid

wooden spoon

MAKES 4 TO 5 SERVINGS

Ask not what your country can do for you—ask what you can do for your country.

LYNDON BAINES

JOHNSON

★ ★

Thirty-sixth President, 1963–1969

Born August 27, 1908, Stonewall, Texas
Died January 22, 1973, Johnson City, Texas

Throughout his life, Lyndon Baines Johnson was known as a masterful politician. He knew how to lead, and he knew how to compromise. When he became president in 1963, he was eager to push through an ambitious program for what he called the Great Society. He achieved much of that program, yet in March 1968, he told a bitterly divided nation that he would not seek reelection. His lofty dreams were shattered by the Vietnam War.

Johnson had grown up in poverty in Texas, working his way through college with a variety of jobs, and he also took time off to teach school. But it was clear that what he really wanted was a career in politics, especially when he came under the spell of President Franklin Roosevelt. Johnson served in the House of Representatives from 1937 to 1948, then in the Senate from 1948 to 1961. Rarely had either branch of Congress seen anyone so skilled in getting legislation passed, and in 1953, he became the youngest majority leader in U.S. Senate history.

Johnson had considerable support in the Democratic Party for the presidential nomination in 1956 and 1960, but he failed to win. When John F. Kennedy won the 1960 nomination, Johnson agreed to be the vice presidential candidate. One reason Kennedy won the election was that Johnson's vigorous campaigning helped many Southerners overcome their doubts about voting for a Catholic for president.

When Kennedy was assassinated in November 1963, President Johnson announced his determination to carry out the slain president's agenda, especially in civil rights. One result was the Civil Rights Act of 1964, barring discrimination in employment and in public facilities such as hotels and restaurants.

During the 1964 election campaign, Johnson announced his plans for the Great Society, inspired by FDR's New Deal. It would include a war on poverty, more civil rights legislation, environmental protection, Medicare and Medicaid, and protection for consumers. The list of Great Society successes was remarkable, including programs such as Head Start, the Office of Economic Opportunity, the Voting Rights Act of 1965, and clean air and clean water acts.

☆ ☆ ☆ ☆ ☆ ☆ ☆ ☆ ☆ ☆ ☆

Family Matters

Johnson liked the initials LBJ, and he was pleased to learn that his wife, the former Claudia Alta Taylor (they were married in 1934), was nicknamed Lady Bird. As Lady Bird Johnson, she had the same initials. The Johnsons carried the theme through in naming their two daughters: Lynda Bird Johnson and Luci Baines Johnson.

Lady Bird Johnson had her own Great Society program to improve the landscape of America, including the Highway Beautification Act of 1965. She traveled 200,000 miles promoting this program, as well as the war on poverty.

☆ ☆ ☆ ☆ ☆ ☆ ☆ ☆ ☆ ☆ ☆

In the 1964 presidential election, Johnson defeated Arizona Republican senator Barry Goldwater, winning 61 percent of the popular vote, the highest percentage of any president in history. One reason for the huge margin was the fear that Goldwater would start bombing Communist North Vietnam. After the election in February 1965, Johnson ordered bombing raids on North Vietnam and committed the first combat troops on the ground. The president was convinced that America must prevent a Communist takeover in Vietnam. As the war continued, however, with ever-increasing death and destruction, more and more Americans became opposed to it.

From 1965 on, the bombing of North Vietnam steadily escalated and so did the number of ground troops in Vietnam. By early 1968, more than 550,000 Americans were in Vietnam, and antiwar protests grew steadily.

In March 1968, Johnson stunned the nation by announcing that he would not seek reelection in November. "How is it possible," he said privately, "that all these people could be so ungrateful to me after I have given them so much?" He retired to his Texas ranch, where he wrote his memoirs and took a hand in the building of the Lyndon Baines Johnson Library. He died of a heart attack in January 1973.

Da-cau: Vietnamese Beanbag Toss

Da-cau is a simple beanbag game that some Americans learned while stationed in Vietnam. You may recognize it as the game of hackeysack. It's a good game for improving coordination, especially for budding soccer stars. Make two beanbags, then practice your skills.

1 Fold the fabric in half with the print sides (or right sides) facing each other.

2 Sew around 2 of the open sides, placing your stitches about ¼ inch from the edge.

3 Turn the beanbag right side out. Fill it a little loosely with dried beans, peas, or rice.

4 Turn the open edges in toward each other and stitch the bag shut. You can use a whipstitch for this, running the thread over the edge, as shown in the drawing.

To play da-cau: The object is to balance the beanbag on the top of your foot without letting it touch the ground. To play, balance a beanbag on your foot, kick it in the air, then catch it on the top of the same foot. Variations include playing with a friend and tossing the bag back and forth, from foot to foot, without letting it touch the ground; or for a contest, each player sees how many times he or she can kick the bag and catch it without letting it touch the ground.

Things You'll Need

cotton fabric, 8 × 5 inches
sewing needle
thread (to match fabric)
scissors
dried beans, dried peas, or rice

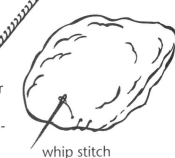
whip stitch

Presidential Pen and Pencil Holder

Things You'll Need

tin can (14–16 ounce)
sheet of white paper or lightweight construction paper
pencil
scissors
transparent tape
white glue or craft glue
sequins, beads, glitter, stars, or any other small decorative items; pumpkin or sunflower
seeds; or small cutouts from construction paper

President Johnson signed an extraordinary number of bills into law, especially as part of his Great Society plan. You might not have to sign your name so many times, but you can use this pen and pencil holder to keep your desktop in order.

1 Place the can (be sure it's clean and dry) on the white paper or construction paper. Use the can as a template to mark its height on the paper. Cut the paper so that it's as wide as the can is high.

2 Tape the edge of the paper to the can and wrap it around the tin. Leave a little overlap and cut off the extra paper. Use either glue or tape to attach the paper firmly to the can.

3 Decorate the pen and pencil holder with small decorative items, different kinds of seeds, or construction paper cutouts. Placement can be haphazard or in a design. Your decorated holder is now ready for pens, pencils, a ruler, and scissors.

In Their Own Words

Our task is to help replace despair with unconditional war on poverty in America.

Richard Milhous Nixon

Thirty-seventh President, 1969–1974

Born *January 9, 1913, Yorba Linda, California*
Died *April 22, 1994, Saddle River, New Jersey*

ichard Milhous Nixon was an opportunist, always looking for ways to advance. Even when he was on his high school debate team in Whittier, California, he had the reputation of using shady tactics to win. Later, while serving in the navy (1942–1946), he was a shrewd poker player and reportedly used his winnings to help finance his first political campaign. Ultimately, Nixon's willingness to use questionable means to reach a desired end would cost him the presidency.

Nixon was elected to the House of Representatives in 1946 and reelected without opposition two years later. He quickly gained a reputation as an anti-Communist crusader, claiming that there were Communist spies in the U.S. government. In 1950, he won a Senate seat by painting his opponent as "soft on Communism." His tactics led one California newspaper to dub him Tricky Dick, and the label stuck.

In 1952, Nixon's anti-Communist stance led to his nomination for vice president on the ticket with Dwight D. Eisenhower. When a newspaper reported that Nixon had a secret slush fund of illegal contributions to help him with campaign expenses, many thought he would have to withdraw from the campaign. Instead, Nixon went on television to explain all the gifts he had received, including a puppy named Checkers. This tearful Checkers speech became famous as an example of Nixon's tactics.

After serving two terms as Eisenhower's vice president, Nixon lost the 1960 presidential election to John F. Kennedy. Two years later, after losing a bid for the governor's chair in California, Nixon's political career seemed to be over. But after Kennedy's death and Johnson's decision not to run in 1968, Nixon ran again and defeated Democrat Hubert Humphrey for the presidency. He was reelected in 1972.

During Nixon's first term, protests against the war in Vietnam reached a fever pitch, especially after Nixon "widened" the conflict into Laos and Cambodia. Incidents such as National Guard troops firing into a crowd of student protesters at Kent State University increased demands for an end to U.S. involvement. And Nixon did withdraw nearly all American troops by late 1972.

Out But Never Down

In spite of the humiliation of being the only president in history to resign, Nixon did not disappear. President Ford granted a "full, free, and absolute pardon" in September 1974, and within a few years, Nixon became something of an elder statesman. He was popular in many foreign countries. After 1980, he had frequent telephone contact with the Reagan administration. His memoirs and articles in magazines revealed his brilliant analyses of current events, especially in foreign affairs. Nixon died in Saddle River, New Jersey, in April 1994.

Family Matters

Thelma Catherine "Pat" Ryan, the future Mrs. Nixon, enjoyed acting and had a bit part in several 1930s films. Nixon, then a young lawyer, auditioned for, and won, a part opposite her in an amateur theatrical performance. The night of the performance, he proposed to her. "I thought he was nuts or something," she recalled, and turned him down. But they did date and married two years later. The Nixons had two daughters, Tricia and Julie.

☆ ☆

A Matter of Timing

In high school and college, Nixon had been a masterful debater. In 1960, he was reluctant to debate John F. Kennedy but finally agreed. Many campaign watchers felt that his poor showing in the televised debates cost Nixon the election. They said he looked pale, tired, and poorly shaved. He may have been fatigued because of a campaign promise to visit all fifty states. When reporters pointed out that there were several states he had missed, Nixon felt obliged to travel to Alaska and other states on the eve of the debate.

☆ ☆

Nixon had some successes, especially in foreign affairs. He made a dramatic trip to Communist China and established more peaceful relations with our Cold War enemy. He also improved relations with the Soviet Union. These successes helped him win reelection in 1972, even though there was already news of the notorious Watergate burglary—a break-in at Democratic Party headquarters that was tied to Nixon's staff.

Month after month, the Nixon administration tried to cover up the affair. The president repeatedly lied, insisting that he knew nothing. Gradually, painfully, the truth emerged. Nixon was partly exposed by his own secret tape recording of meetings in his office. On August 8, 1974, he resigned his office rather than face impeachment proceedings. A dozen of those working closest to the president received prison terms.

Moon Cakes

This tasty recipe seems a fitting tribute to President Nixon. First, moon cakes are a traditional treat at the annual Moon Festival, held in China every autumn, and Nixon's 1972 trip to China was one of the great achievements of his presidency. Second, in July 1969, he was on board the aircraft carrier that picked up the *Apollo* astronauts following the historic landing on the moon—another highlight of the Nixon administration.

1 Have an adult preheat the oven to 375 degrees F.

2 In a large bowl, use an egg beater or mixer to cream the butter. Add the butter and the sugar to the egg yolk in a large bowl and stir until creamy.

3 Add the flour and salt. Stir well to mix thoroughly. Form the dough into a ball, wrap it in aluminum foil, and refrigerate for at least 30 minutes.

4 When the dough is chilled, take it out of the refrigerator and remove the foil.

5 Break off pieces of dough and mold each piece into a small ball (or moon). Use your thumb to make a depression in each moon cake, and fill each hole with a little jam. You can add a few sesame seeds if you wish for more of a Chinese flavor.

6 Place the moon cakes on a baking sheet and bake at 375 degrees F for 20 minutes.

7 Have an adult use oven mitts to take the baking sheet out of the oven and put it on a cooling rack.

Things You'll Need

½ cup (1 stick) unsalted butter at room temperature
¼ cup sugar
1 egg yolk
1 cup all-purpose flour
¼ teaspoon salt
¼ cup jam—any flavor
sesame seeds (optional)
adult helper
measuring cup
measuring spoon
large bowl
egg beater or mixer
wooden spoon
aluminum foil
teaspoon
baking sheet
oven mitts
cooling rack
MAKES 12 TO 18 MOON CAKES

Word Search

The puzzle shows ten words associated with Richard Nixon. Find all ten, drawing a line around each. Remember that words (or names) can read left to right; right to left; up, down, or on the diagonal.

POKER	WATERGATE	VIETNAM
CHECKERS	RESIGN	NAVY
BREAK-IN	DEBATE	CHINA
IMPEACH		

```
L  K  M  N  I  E  B  Y  C  N  L  A
D  B  W  A  T  E  R  G  A  T  E  B
V  A  N  R  E  K  C  H  S  I  G  Y
I  P  A  C  H  M  A  L  T  E  I  V
M  V  I  M  N  E  B  M  K  Y  C  A
P  C  H  D  E  B  A  T  E  N  H  N
E  O  R  A  I  N  V  Y  G  W  E  B
A  B  K  N  T  R  M  I  A  D  C  L
C  A  M  E  N  Z  S  C  N  R  K  I
H  D  I  B  R  E  A  K  I  N  E  L
B  V  J  N  R  I  S  E  H  B  R  D
E  C  L  M  T  E  V  R  C  L  S  A
```

Answers appear at the back of the book.

I let the American people down, and I have to carry that burden with me for the rest of my life.

GERALD RUDOLPH FORD

Thirty-eighth President, 1974–1977

Born *July 14, 1913, Omaha, Nebraska*

L ate in his distinguished career in Congress, Gerald R. Ford seemed content with life. He was happily married, the father of three sons and a daughter, and regarded as a congressman's congressman. In the early 1970s, his one remaining ambition was to be Speaker of the House of Representatives. Instead, he became president of the United States.

Ford was born in Omaha, Nebraska. Following the divorce of his parents when he was two, he moved with his mother to Grand Rapids, Michigan. After high school, he became an outstanding football player at the University of Michigan (1931–1935). He earned a law degree from Yale and practiced law until World War II. He served in the navy (1942–1946) and saw action on a light aircraft carrier in the Pacific.

In 1948, Ford was elected to Congress and won reelection twelve more times, always with more than 60 percent of the vote. From 1948 to 1973, he was one of the Republican leaders of the House and was one of the two House members to serve on the Warren Commission, investigating the assassination of President Kennedy. He set his sights on becoming Speaker of the House and was elected minority leader in 1965 (he could become speaker only when the Republicans had a majority).

In 1973, Vice President Spiro Agnew, facing charges of corruption, resigned. Ford was appointed to replace him. He was confirmed in the Senate by a vote of 93 to 3. Less than a year later, on August 9, 1974, Nixon resigned and Ford became president, the first to serve without being chosen in a national election.

One of President Ford's first acts was to grant Richard Nixon a full pardon in September 1974, hoping it would spare the nation a long, ugly court trial. But the pardon triggered a storm of protest, and Ford never recovered his popularity. His administration was also hampered by the country's gloomy mood resulting from the Watergate crisis, by persistent inflation (increases in the cost of living), and by the final Communist triumph in Vietnam. In 1975, in two isolated incidents, attempts were made to assassi-

An Athletic Hunk

Gerald Ford had been an outstanding athlete in high school, and several colleges tried to sign him. He ended up with Michigan, became a star center on the football team, and was named most valuable player in 1934. When the College All-Stars played the professional Chicago Bears on New Year's Day 1935, Ford played both defense and offense, staying in the game for fifty-eight of the sixty minutes. After graduation, he was hired as assistant football coach and head boxing coach at Yale University, and he then went into law.

In the late 1930s, the rugged-looking Jerry Ford tried modeling for a time, appearing in a *Look* magazine spread on winter sports and then in his navy uniform on the cover of *Cosmopolitan* in 1942.

Family Matters

Ford did not marry until he was thirty-five. His bride, thirty-year-old Eliza-beth Anne Bloomer, was a dancer trained by the famous Martha Graham. The Fords had four children: Michael, Jack, Steven, and Susan. As first lady, Betty Ford spoke often in favor of women's rights. After recovering from breast cancer, she was widely praised for her candid discussion of what had been a hush-hush topic. Then after becoming addicted to pain relievers and alcohol while trying to find relief for an inoperable pinched nerve, she again had the courage to talk openly about her struggles. She lent her name to the creation of the Betty Ford Clinic for treatment of substance dependence.

nate Ford, each time by a woman, and each time the woman fired a revolver and missed. Both would-be assassins went to prison.

The nation's mood and Ford's reputation received a big boost from the country's bicentennial in 1976. Ford was thrilled to preside over the five-day festivities that featured "tall ships" (sailing vessels) from more than thirty countries on parade in New York Harbor. Later that year, Ford ran for reelection but was defeated by Jimmy Carter.

Bicentennial Strawberry Shortcake

"Never in my wildest dreams," President Ford wrote, "had I imagined that I would be president of the United States on its two hundredth birthday." He was thrilled to be part of the celebration. What better way to mark the event than with his favorite food: strawberry shortcake.

1 Have an adult preheat the oven to 425 degrees F.

2 Rinse the strawberries under cold running water and drain in a colander or large strainer. With an adult's help, hull the berries, slice them, and place them in a small bowl. Add sugar and stir until the berries are the sweetness you like. Set aside.

3 Butter an 8-inch cake pan and lightly sprinkle it with flour.

4 Mix the flour, baking powder, salt, and sugar in a large bowl. Use a pastry blender or your fingers to cut bits of the butter into the flour mixture until it looks like coarse meal.

5 Slowly stir in the milk. Use just enough to hold the dough together.

6 Sprinkle a little flour on a pastry board or cloth and turn the dough onto it. Knead the dough for 1 or 2 minutes, then put it in the cake pan, patting it flat with your hand. Bake for 12 to 15 minutes at 425 degrees F.

7 Have an adult use oven mitts to remove the shortcake from the oven. While still warm, cut it into 8 wedges. Cut the wedges in half horizontally, butter them, and fill with the strawberries. Top with lots of whipped cream.

 **Things You'll Need**

1 pint strawberries
sugar to sprinkle on berries
butter and flour for pan
2 cups all-purpose flour
4 teaspoons baking powder
1 teaspoon salt
1½ tablespoons sugar
5 tablespoons unsalted butter
⅔ cup milk
whipped cream
adult helper
measuring cup
measuring spoon
colander or strainer
paring knife
cutting board
small bowl
wooden spoon
8-inch round cake pan
large bowl
pastry blender (or your fingers)
pastry board or cloth
table knife
oven mitts
MAKES 8 SERVINGS

Quotation Formation

Figure out answers to the clues, and write the letters on the numbered spaces. Some of the letters from a clue can be used in more than one answer. Transfer each letter to the blank quote at the bottom to discover something President Ford said.

Clues	**Words**
1 Ford attended the _____ Academy.	1 $\overline{~}~\overline{~}~\overline{~}~\overline{~}~\overline{~}$ $\quad$ 8 $\quad$ 22 $\quad$ 28 $\quad$ 14 $\quad$ 4
2 He used his presidential power to _____ bills.	2 $\overline{~}~\overline{~}~\overline{~}~\overline{~}$ $\quad$ 28 $\quad$ 29 $\quad$ 10 $\quad$ 1
3 Ford wanted to be Speaker of the _____.	3 $\overline{~}~\overline{~}~\overline{~}~\overline{~}~\overline{~}$ $\quad$ 19 $\quad$ 5 $\quad$ 2 $\quad$ 26 $\quad$ 24
4 In college he was an outstanding _____.	4 $\overline{~}~\overline{~}~\overline{~}~\overline{~}~\overline{~}~\overline{~}~\overline{~}$ $\quad$ 9 $\quad$ 20 $\quad$ 19 $\quad$ 15 $\quad$ 29 $\quad$ 10 $\quad$ 24
5 Ford did not believe that _____ makes right.	5 $\overline{~}~\overline{~}~\overline{~}~\overline{~}~\overline{~}$ $\quad$ 21 $\quad$ 11 $\quad$ 18 $\quad$ 19 $\quad$ 10
6 He came from the Midwest _____ of the country.	6 $\overline{~}~\overline{~}~\overline{~}~\overline{~}~\overline{~}~\overline{~}$ $\quad$ 23 $\quad$ 24 $\quad$ 7 $\quad$ 17 $\quad$ 27 $\quad$ 16
7 Playing both offense and defense made Ford a man of _____.	7 $\overline{~}~\overline{~}~\overline{~}~\overline{~}$ $\quad$ 25 $\quad$ 30 $\quad$ 12 $\quad$ 13
8 Ford _____ for reelection in 1976.	8 $\overline{~}~\overline{~}~\overline{~}$ $\quad$ 3 $\quad$ 9 $\quad$ 6

" $\overline{~}~\overline{~}~\overline{~}~~\overline{~}~\overline{~}~\overline{~}~\overline{~}~~\overline{~}~\overline{~}~\overline{~}~\overline{~}~\overline{~}~\overline{~}~\overline{~}~\overline{~}$
$\quad$ 1 $\quad$ 2 $\quad$ 3 $\quad\quad$ 4 $\quad$ 5 $\quad$ 6 $\quad$ 7 $\quad\quad$ 8 $\quad$ 9 $\quad$ 10 $\quad$ 11 $\quad$ 12 $\quad$ 13 $\quad$ 14 $\quad$ 15

$\overline{~}~\overline{~}~\overline{~}~\overline{~}~\overline{~}~\overline{~}~\overline{~}~\overline{~}~\overline{~}~~\overline{~}~\overline{~}~~\overline{~}~\overline{~}~\overline{~}~\overline{~}$ "
$\quad$ 16 $\quad$ 17 $\quad$ 18 $\quad$ 19 $\quad$ 20 $\quad$ 21 $\quad$ 22 $\quad$ 23 $\quad$ 24 $\quad\quad$ 25 $\quad$ 26 $\quad\quad$ 27 $\quad$ 28 $\quad$ 29 $\quad$ 30

Answers appear at the back of the book.

In Their Own WORDS

My fellow Americans, our long national nightmare is over.

JIMMY (JAMES EARL) CARTER, JR.

Thirty-ninth President, 1977–1981

Born *October 1, 1924, Plains, Georgia*

When Jimmy Carter ran for president in 1976, many people did not know who he was. Questions like "Jimmy Who?" and "President of What?" were frequent refrains throughout the campaign. That lack of knowledge about the man turned out to be an asset. Americans were fed up with the Watergate scandal, and they found it refreshing that Carter had no deep roots in Washington. He tried to bring the presidency closer to the American people with informal "fireside talks" similar to those of Franklin Roosevelt and with frank discussion of the nation's problems.

Carter presented himself as a simple, small-town Georgian who made his living as a peanut farmer. But he was actually a complex man and an ambitious one. After attending Georgia Tech, he went to the U.S. Naval Academy, graduating in 1946. During his navy career, he studied nuclear physics at Union College and was chosen by Admiral Hyman Rickover, the father of nuclear submarines, to serve as engineer on the *Sea Wolf*, one of the first nuclear submarines.

Following the death of his father in 1953, Carter left the navy to take over the family businesses, which included growing peanuts, warehousing, and processing cotton. He was an intelligent businessman and became wealthy. He entered politics in 1962, winning election to the Georgia Senate, where he served until 1967. He was then elected governor on his second try in 1970.

He was a surprise candidate for the Democratic nomination for president. One reason for his victory over Gerald Ford was that Ford had been appointed by Nixon and then pardoned him. Carter's single term in the White House was a stormy one, as the nation was rocked by events over which he had little or no control. The soaring inflation of the 1970s continued, for example, and government measures did little to ease it. He was also severely criticized for several well-intentioned decisions. One of his first presidential acts was to grant a full pardon to ten thousand young men who had avoided the draft during the Vietnam War. While many people cheered the decision, war veterans were furious. And when the Soviet Union invaded Afghanistan, Carter felt a strong response was important. But halting grain shipments to the Soviet Union upset American farmers, and his decision to join sixty-three other nations in a boycott of the 1980 Olympic Games in Moscow hurt his reputation even more.

Family Matters

Jimmy Carter married soon after his graduation from the Naval Academy. He was twenty-one and Rosalynn Smith was eighteen. She had been an excellent student in high school and college. As first lady, she frequently discussed issues with her husband. Because she was from the South but also tough, the White House staff nicknamed her Steel Magnolia. Her memoir, *First Lady from Plains* (1984) was a best-seller.

The Carters had three sons (John, James, and Jeffrey) and one daughter, Amy, who was nine when they moved to the White House. Her pet Siamese cat was named Misty Malarky Yin Yang.

The Carter administration did enjoy some important successes, including a strong stance on human rights throughout the world. Carter also played a key role in the 1978 Camp David Accords, which established peace between Egypt and Israel for the first time in thirty years. Carter was awarded the 2002 Nobel Peace Prize for his work. But his chances of winning reelection in 1980 were crushed by the Iran Hostage Crisis. Militant factions in Iran held fifty-two Americans hostage for a total of 444 days. The failure of the president to gain their release was seen as a sign of his weakness. The final humiliation was the release of the hostages on the day Ronald Reagan took the oath of office as the next president.

You'll Need

adult helper

avocado pit (avocados are available in supermarkets)

4 toothpicks

9- or 12 ounce glass (or plastic cup)

tap water

Plant Nursery

During his presidency and after, Carter was devoted to several causes: protecting the environment, conserving energy, working for peace and for human rights. After his term in office, he led by example; for instance, he promoted Habitat for Humanity by putting on a carpenter's apron and actually worked at building houses for low-income people. In schools, he and Rosalynn encouraged children to recycle and to grow things. This activity provides a way to start a plant.

1 Clean the fruit thoroughly off the avocado pit.

2 Poke 4 toothpicks into the middle part of the pit so that it will remain suspended in the glass.

3 Suspend the avocado in the glass with the pointed end of the pit facing up.

4 Add water so that the pit is half covered. Keep the water at that level throughout the activity.

5 Place the glass in a sunny location. Be patient. Within 7 to 10 days, the pit will crack open and a plant will emerge, as well as roots from the bottom.

6 When the roots seem solid, you can transplant the avocado in a large pot or a garden.

☆ ☆

The Law of Averages

Until late in the twentieth century, none of the nation's presidents had served in the navy. A number had been generals in the army: Washington, Jackson, William Henry Harrison, Taylor, Pierce, Andrew Johnson, Grant, Hayes, Garfield, Arthur, Benjamin Harrison, and Eisenhower. It wasn't until John F. Kennedy that the first navy man made it to the White House. After JFK, Johnson, Nixon, Ford, and Carter brought the score to a more respectable Army 12, Navy 5.

☆ ☆

Georgia Peanut Brittle

Not surprisingly, peanuts were one of President Carter's favorite foods. Here is a tasty recipe for peanut brittle.

1 Butter the bottom and sides of the baking pan. Place the sugar in a saucepan. Add the vanilla and lemon extracts.

2 Melt the sugar mixture over medium heat, stirring constantly with a wooden spoon.

3 When the sugar has melted into a thin syrup, turn off the heat and add the peanuts. Stir vigorously, then quickly pour the mixture into the baking pan.

4 While the brittle is still warm, have an adult help you use a knife to mark it into squares. *Hint:* If the knife begins to stick, quickly run hot water over it.

5 When the peanut brittle has cooled, remove it from the pan. Break it into pieces along the marked lines. Store it in a covered glass container.

Things You'll Need

butter for baking pan
2 cups sugar
½ teaspoon vanilla extract
½ teaspoon lemon extract
1 cup roasted peanuts, chopped. (For another Southern treat, you can use the same recipe with 1 cup sesame seeds.)
adult helper
measuring cup
measuring spoon
9 inch baking pan
2 quart saucepan
wooden spoon
sharp knife
glass container with lid
MAKES 1 POUND

Human rights is the soul of our foreign policy.

RONALD WILSON
REAGAN

* *

Fortieth President, 1981–1989

Born *February 6, 1911, Tampico, Illinois*
Died *June 5, 2004, Bel Air, California*

alfway through his two terms as president, Ronald Reagan declared, "It's morning again in America!" The important thing about that statement was that Reagan believed it—and so did the majority of the American people. The man they called the Great Communicator had a remarkable ability to persuade people to believe in themselves and in their country.

Reagan had been sharpening his persuasive skills for more than fifty years by the time he became president. As a boy growing up in a small town in Illinois, for example, Reagan convinced officials that the town needed a lifeguard, and he held down the job for the next seven summers. At Eureka College, he persuaded the football coach to let him play, although he was woefully nearsighted. And after graduating in 1932, he talked a radio station into letting him broadcast football and baseball games. Over the next five years, he became famous for his radio broadcasts. Relying only on telegraph reports, Reagan was able to describe the game as if he was there, using sound effects such as recorded crowd noises.

Reagan went on to have a successful movie career, acting in about fifty films between 1937 and 1965, usually as the clean-cut pal who never got the girl. One of his most memorable roles was in a comedy called *Bedtime for Bonzo*, in which he played opposite a chimp. In the 1960s, he was host of a General Electric television series, and millions of Americans became familiar with his warm personality and his soft, pleasing voice. Traveling the country for GE helped to transform Reagan from a liberal Democrat to a pro-business Republican.

In 1966, Reagan entered politics for the first time. He was elected governor of California and reelected four years later. He was a popular governor, credited with reducing the state's debt and reforming the welfare system. His success led him to try for the Republican presidential nomination. After failing to win the nomination three times, he finally won it in 1980 and beat Democrat Jimmy Carter for the presidency. He was sixty-nine years old, the oldest elected president. He was also the only professional actor to become president.

Joking under Fire

In March 1981, President Reagan and three others were shot and seriously wounded by a would-be assassin. As he was being wheeled into emergency surgery, he spotted Mrs. Reagan. "Honey, I forgot to duck," he said. Moments later, in the operating room, he gestured toward the surgeons who were about to remove the bullet lodged within an inch of his heart. "I hope you're all Republicans," he quipped.

Throughout his two terms in the White House, Reagan remained one of the most popular presidents. His record, however, was mixed. The inflation rate was cut in half and more new jobs were created than at any time in the nation's history. Taxes were cut, too. But the improved economy came at a high price: the nation's debt soared past $1 trillion and then doubled by the time he left office. And the Reagan tax cuts turned out to benefit only the very wealthy. In addition, Americans were shocked to learn that the president had approved a secret sale of weapons to Iran. But even this Iran-Contra scandal did little to lessen his popularity.

After leaving office in 1989, President Reagan and First Lady Nancy Reagan retired to their ranch in California. In the 1990s, Reagan announced that he was suffering from Alzheimer's disease and succumbed to the illness in June 2004.

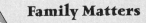

Family Matters

Ronald Reagan was first married to Jane Wyman from 1940 to 1948. He and Jane had two children, Maureen and Michael. In 1952, Reagan married Nancy Davis, another actress. They also had two children, Patricia Ann and Ronald Prescott. Few first couples have had a more loving relationship than Ronald and Nancy Reagan. As first lady, Nancy became a leader of antidrug campaigns and was best known for the Just Say No program. Her book, *My Turn*, published in 1989, describes her years in the White House.

Reagan Bean Jar

Ronald Reagan's favorite treat was jelly beans, and there was always a jar on the table at every meeting. (The president picked out all coconut-flavored jelly beans for himself.) In this project, you'll make an attractive jar of layered beans as a tribute to the fortieth president. Instead of jelly beans, however, you'll make your decorative jar with dried beans, peas, and lentils.

1 Arrange your dried foods on your work surface. Choose one for the bottom layer. Spoon a bean layer into the jar. Make the layer about 1 inch deep.

2 Spoon other layers on top of the first. Don't stir.

3 Continue alternating layers until the jar is full.

4 For an added touch, place a piece of fabric over the top, then screw on the lid over the fabric. Use your bean jar as a paperweight or simply as a decorative object.

Things You'll Need

various dried beans such as lentils, peas, navy beans, kidney beans (you can make one layer of jelly beans if you want to)

spoon

1-quart glass jar with lid

piece of print fabric, about 4 inches square

☆ ☆

"Win One for the Gipper"

President Reagan's favorite movie role was in a 1940 film, *Knute Rockne—All-American*, about Notre Dame's famous football coach. Reagan played the part of a star player named George Gipp, nicknamed Gipper. In a classic deathbed scene, the terminally ill player says to the coach, "Someday, when things are tough, maybe you can ask the boys to go in there and win just once for the Gipper."

During Reagan's political campaigns, "Win one for the Gipper" became a common slogan.

☆ ☆

Star Wars Styrofoam Mobile

Things You'll Need

pencil
sheet of white paper
several thin Styrofoam trays
    from supermarkets
crayon or felt-tip pen
scissors
hole punch
glow-in-the-dark paints
black or white thread
coat hanger

As president, Reagan wanted to build a complex missile-defense system to be placed in Earth's orbit where it would be used to destroy any missiles fired at the United States. Critics labeled the plan Star Wars and said it was nothing more than a fantasy. As a tribute to this space-age idea, here's a project for making a Star Wars mobile out of recycled Styrofoam.

1 Draw some space shapes, such as stars, planets, astronauts, and space-ships, on a sheet of paper.

2 Copy the forms onto the Styrofoam using a crayon or felt-tip pen. Cut out the shapes.

3 Use the hole punch to make a hole in the top of each shape. Add any details with crayon, pen, or glowing paints.

4 Tie different lengths of thread through the holes, then attach each piece to the coat hanger. Experiment with different placement and lengths of thread until you're pleased with the effect.

In Their Own Words

> What I'd really like to do is go down in history as the President who made Americans believe in themselves again.

GEORGE HERBERT WALKER BUSH

Forty-first President, 1989–1993

Born *June 12, 1924, Milton, Massachusetts*

George Herbert Walker Bush was very ambitious. Partly because of this drive to succeed, his presidency was marked by highs and lows. He was particularly successful in building a coalition of allies before sending U.S. forces into the Gulf War in 1991.

Bush grew up in Connecticut (with summers in Maine) as a member of a wealthy family. As a student, he excelled in academics and in sports. He was team captain in high school baseball, soccer, and basketball, as well as captain of his Yale baseball team. In June 1942, he graduated from high school, turned eighteen, and enlisted in the U.S. Navy, eager to take part in World War II as a pilot. He became the navy's youngest pilot and flew fifty-eight missions. In September 1944, his fighter-bomber was shot down by Japanese antiaircraft fire. After his two surviving crewmen bailed out, Bush followed and was picked up by an American submarine. He was awarded the Distinguished Flying Cross for heroism.

After the war, Bush married Barbara Pierce and graduated from Yale in less than three years. Bush moved to Texas in 1948 and joined with friends in forming two oil companies, which rapidly made him a millionaire. By the early 1960s, he felt ready to switch to politics. His father, Prescott Bush, retired in 1963 after serving ten years as a U.S. senator from Connecticut.

In 1964, running as the Texas Republican candidate for the U.S. Senate, Bush was defeated. But two years later, he won a seat in the House of Representatives and served two terms. After failing in another bid for the Senate in 1970, he was appointed to a succession of offices by President Nixon and then by President Ford.

Bush's broad experience and leadership in the Republican Party led him to be selected as Ronald Reagan's running mate in 1980. During his eight years as vice president, Bush traveled widely, logging in more than a million miles and visiting fifty countries. In 1988, Bush was elected president, defeating Democrat Michael Dukakis.

Eat Your . . .

Bush had a powerful dislike of broccoli and banned it from the White House kitchen. He said, "I'm the president of the United States, and I'm not going to eat any more broccoli." Growers then sent truckloads of the vegetable to the White House.

Family Matters

Although George and Barbara Bush came from wealthy families, their desire to strike out on their own led to some hard times and frequent moves. They occupied twenty-nine homes in seventeen cities. The Bushes had four sons, George, who became the forty-third president, Jeb, Neil, and Marvin, and a daughter, Dorothy; another daughter, Robin, died in childhood.

As first lady, Barbara Bush promoted adult literacy. She also gave her support to programs for the homeless and for children, including Head Start. Her two humorous books, written from the point of view of the family dogs, made the best-seller list.

Who's on First?

In college, Bush was captain of the baseball team, played first base, and batted .280. In his junior and senior years, his Yale team made it to the college world series. He also played on the varsity soccer team while earning academic honors.

The four years of Bush's presidency were like a roller-coaster ride. The collapse of Communism in Europe between 1989 and 1991 was an exciting time, as country after country ended Communist dictatorships and established democracies. In 1991, after Iraqi forces invaded Kuwait, the United States led a coalition of countries in a lightning-fast victory over Saddam Hussein's forces. President Bush briefly enjoyed the greatest approval rating of any modern president.

But Bush could not overcome a series of unpopular decisions, such as failing to live up to his promise of "no new taxes." The economy grew steadily worse, and in 1992, Bush lost his bid for a second term. He retired and assumed the role of elder statesman.

Basketball Bead Game

Things You'll Need

black felt-tip pen

small paper or plastic cup (the kind used to hold ketchup in many cafeterias or fast-food restaurants)

wooden bead, ¾-inch or 1 inch, with hole

acrylic paint (burnt orange)

paintbrush

large thumbtack

14-inch dowel, ¼- or ⅜-inch diameter

white glue

screw eye

about 20 inches of yarn or string

In recognition of George Bush's skill in basketball (and other sports), this project offers a mini-basketball game that's fun to make and to play. It's also good practice for hand-eye coordination.

1 Use a felt-tip pen to make cross-hatch lines on the sides of the paper cup to look like the netting of a basketball net.

2 To give the bead the look of a basketball, paint it with burnt orange acrylic paint. When the paint is dry, draw lines on the "ball" with the pen like the lines on a basketball.

3 Push a thumbtack through the cup from the inside and press it into the dowel near the top, with the top of the cup even with the top of the dowel. For a firmer hold, add a little white glue to the dowel before you press the thumbtack in place.

4 Insert the screw eye about 3 inches below the top of the dowel, on the opposite side from the basket. Tie one end of the yarn or string to the screw eye.

5 Push the other end of the yarn through the bead basketball and tie it in place.

6 Your game is ready to play. After some practice tosses, make it a contest with a friend or by yourself. See how many baskets you can make in every 10 tries.

Oil and Water Experiment

In 1989, President Bush sent troops to Alaska to help clean up the worst oil spill in America's history. An oil tanker, the *Exxon Valdez*, had run aground on offshore rocks, disgorging 10.8 million gallons of oil, covering the delicate beach ecosystem. Over the next few weeks, Americans had a painful lesson in how oil spreads in water and its devastating effect on plant and animal life. In this simple experiment, you can demonstrate how oil floats on water and coats anything that touches it, then use your creation as an interesting display.

Things You'll Need

measuring cup
measuring spoon
1-quart jar or bottle with lid, clear glass or plastic (a seltzer bottle with a cap works well)
tap water
funnel
2 tablespoons salt
1 cup salad oil
craft stick or dowel
blue food coloring
glitter—silver or gold

1 Fill the jar or bottle with 3 cups of water. Use the funnel to add the salt. Cover and shake until the salt is dissolved.

2 Add the salad oil to the bottle using the funnel. Put the lid on, shake the bottle, then let it sit for 1 or 2 minutes. What happens to the oil after it's mixed with water?

3 Place a dowel or craft stick in the bottle for a few minutes, then pull it out. The craft stick will be coated with oil. In the same way, thousands of sea otters, bald eagles, and other wildlife were coated with oil from the *Exxon Valdez*, and they died.

4 Turn your experiment into an ocean display by adding a few drops of blue food coloring and a little glitter. Tighten the cap or lid, and lay the bottle on its side. Tip it gently back and forth to create the effect of waves.

In Their Own WORDS

We as a people have such a purpose today. It is to make kinder the face of the nation and gentler the face of the world.

BILL (WILLIAM JEFFERSON) CLINTON

Forty-second President, 1993–2001

Born *August 19, 1946, Hope, Arkansas*

In 1963, high school student Bill Clinton was chosen to attend a national conference called Boys' Nation in Washington, D.C. At the White House, he met and shook hands with President John F. Kennedy, his idol. He had already decided on a career in politics, and this was the highlight of his boyhood. When he was elected to the presidency in 1992, he was determined to live up to his image of Kennedy. He enjoyed considerable success in both economic policies and foreign relations decisions.

Clinton grew up in a troubled home with an abusive stepfather, but he was still an excellent student, both in high school and in college at Georgetown University in Washington, D.C. He served as an intern for Arkansas senator William Fulbright and also won a Rhodes Scholarship for a year's study in England, where he joined in protests against America's war in Vietnam.

After graduating from Yale Law School, Clinton launched his political career and married Hillary Rodham. He lost a bid for a seat in Congress, but in 1978 he became the youngest governor in Arkansas history at age thirty-two. His term was a disaster. People found him to be arrogant and overly ambitious. After losing his bid for a second term in 1980, a more humble Clinton asked the voters for another chance in 1982. In his second term, he became one of the nation's most popular governors, winning widespread acclaim for reforming schools in Arkansas.

In 1992, Clinton ran for president with Tennessee's Al Gore as vice president, forming the youngest team of candidates in history. Clinton won the presidency over incumbent George Bush. Clinton easily won reelection in 1996 over Senator Bob Dole of Kansas.

Clinton's two terms in the White House were remarkable for both their successes and their failures. He had campaigned on promises to improve the economy, correct poor decisions made by his Republican predecessors, and reduce the nation's debt. By the time he left office in 2001, the United States had enjoyed the longest economic expansion in history, along with the lowest unemployment rate in thirty years and the highest rate ever of new jobs created. His reform of welfare was also popular. His budgets not only ended the huge deficit but actually produced a surplus. In foreign policy he worked for peace, especially in Ireland and the Middle

Many Talents

Clinton had a gift as a musician and played the saxophone with energy. He often played during political campaigns and was seen on television shows performing.

East, and sent U.S. troops into the former Yugoslavia as part of a United Nations peacekeeping effort.

Unfortunately, Clinton's reputation was seriously damaged by a series of personal mistakes and scandals. He and First Lady Hillary Rodham Clinton were accused of financial wrongdoing in a real estate deal called Whitewater. More troubling were reports of a sexual relationship between Clinton and a young White House intern. He was impeached by the House but acquitted by the Senate. One of the most amazing things about Clinton was that he remained popular even though he admitted to his wrongdoing. When he left office in 2001, he wrote his memoirs, supported Hillary's successful campaign as a Democratic senator from New York, and raised record sums for the Democratic Party. He continues to work for welfare reform through-out the nation, as well as for many other causes around the world.

Presidential Diet

Throughout his life, Clinton was, as he put it, a fast-food junkie. He put on too much weight, his health suffered, and he was forced to have heart bypass surgery. After leaving the White House, he started a campaign to improve Americans' eating habits.

Arkansas Berry Basket

Bill Clinton is proud of his Arkansas heritage, which includes an array of handcrafts still produced by hundreds of craftspeople, especially those living in the state's Ozark Mountains. Baskets are usually made with thin strips of wood that craft workers weave into beautiful and sturdy shapes. For your Arkansas berry basket, you'll use lightweight poster board.

Things You'll Need

2 sheets of lightweight poster board in 2 different colors, each 12 × 24 inches
ruler
pencil
scissors
stapler
white glue
7 or 8 paper clips

1 Let's say we're using green and brown poster board. With a ruler and pencil, mark a strip on the brown poster board 1 inch wide and 24 inches long. Cut it out with scissors.

2 Use the strip to mark and cut out 11 more brown strips, for a total of 12.

3 Repeat steps 1 and 2 to make 12 green strips.

4 Place 4 strips on your work surface, alternating the 2 colors, as shown. Push the strips together so that there is no space between them. Put a staple in each of the 4 corners.

5 Fold all 16 unwoven ends up to start the sides. See drawing.

6 Weave 2 green strips and 2 brown strips in and out of the side strips. Overlap the ends and hold them in place with a little glue. (Use paper clips to hold the overlap in place until the glue dries.)

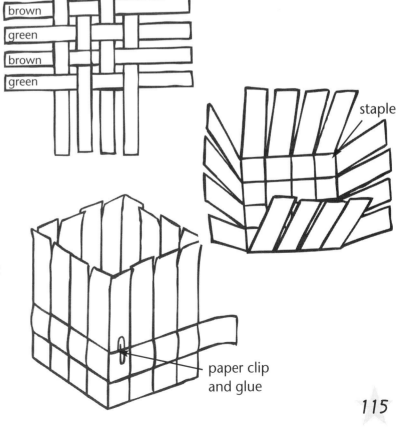

brown
green
brown
green

staple

paper clip and glue

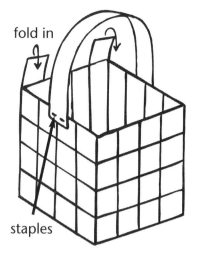

fold in

staples

President Clinton and First Lady Hillary Clinton formed a close working partnership unlike anything seen in American politics. This tight relationship alarmed critics when Hillary was given an office in the West Wing of the White House, which is normally reserved for senior presidential advisers. When she was placed at the head of the National Health Reform Task Force, the criticism reached a fever pitch. The recommendations of the task force were rejected by Congress, sinking one of President Clinton's most important programs. The Clintons and their daughter, Chelsea, weathered these storms, as well as those arising from the personal scandals. After leaving the White House, the first lady was elected to the U.S. Senate from New York.

☆☆☆☆☆☆☆☆☆☆

7 When all 4 side strips have been woven, bend the upright ends inside the basket and glue them in place.

8 You can add a handle by making an extra strip of poster board, arch it over the basket, and staple it in place.

Name and Word Detection

For each clue, write the answer on the five blank spaces. Spell the word with five of the six scrambled letters on that line. Place the sixth, or extra, letter in the last column. The letters in that last column, when unscrambled, will spell out the name of a U.S. president.

1 Clinton served two of them. _ _ _ _ _   T M R N E S _

2 The color of his house for eight years was _____. _ _ _ _ _   H I T W J E _

3 Clinton was involved in a real estate scandal called White _____. _ _ _ _ _   R H W T E A _

4 The branch of Congress that impeached Clinton. _ _ _ _ _   S N U O E H _

5 The people _____ a president every four years. _ _ _ _ _   L O E T C E _

6 You have to be eighteen to be one. _ _ _ _ _   T O R E V O _

7 Clinton worked for _____ in the world. _ _ _ _ _   C P A S E E _

8 _ _ _ _ _ _ _ _

Answers appear at the back of the book.

In Their Own WORDS

There is nothing wrong with America that cannot be cured by what is right with America.

116

George Walker Bush

Forty-third President, 2001–

Born *July 6, 1946, New Haven, Connecticut*

For the first forty years of his life, George W. Bush might have been voted least likely to become president of the United States. He surprised everyone by becoming a successful campaigner and a popular president. His two terms in the White House were punctuated by the 9/11 attack on the World Trade Center and the Pentagon and by his decision to invade Iraq. His response to both events convinced many that he was a forceful and determined leader.

In high school and at Yale, Bush had passing grades, but he was more interested in sports and having fun. He joined the Air National Guard in 1973 to avoid the draft during the Vietnam War, and he earned a master's degree in business in 1975. Throughout his thirties, however, he could not seem to find a career. He was devoted to his father, George Herbert Walker Bush, and helped in his successful presidential campaign. He also had an up-and-down record in the Texas oil business.

In 1977, he tried running for Congress but lost. "Defeat humbles you," he admitted later. "Frankly, getting whipped was probably a pretty good thing for me," Bush said. In the mid-1980s, Bush began to change. He rededicated himself to his religion with the help of evangelist Billy Graham. He gave up alcohol and cigarettes. In 1988, he played an important part in his father's presidential election. A year later, he became part owner and managing partner of the Texas Rangers major league baseball team. He loved baseball and quickly became a successful, highly visible owner who was well known throughout the state.

In 1994, Bush decided to run for political office again, this time for Texas governor. He ran a brilliant campaign against the well-liked governor Ann Richardson and won the election. He was a popular governor and won a second term with nearly 70 percent of the vote.

With the help and support of his father and his father's friends, Bush ran for president in 2000. Dick Cheney, who had served in his father's cabinet, was the candidate for vice president. The Bush-Cheney team won in one of the closest and most controversial elections in history. In Florida, where Bush's younger brother, Jeb, was governor, Bush won by a mere five hundred votes.

Family Matters

Bush's first date with his future wife, Laura, was a round of miniature golf. After their marriage a few months later, they had no honeymoon because he was campaigning for Congress. George and Laura have twin girls, Jenna and Barbara. In the 1990s, Laura Bush became a literacy advocate and helped organize the Texas Book Festival, a celebration of Texas books and authors; it has been an annual event since 1996. As first lady, she has continued to promote literacy programs and women's health issues, especially breast cancer awareness.

A recount, because of questionable ballots, was stopped by a Supreme Court decision, which gave the state—and the election—to Bush. Many Democrats felt they'd been the victims of another "stolen" election (see the chapter on Rutherford B. Hayes).

Bush's first term in the White House was highlighted by two decisions with far-reaching consequences. First, the terrorist attacks of September 11, 2001, propelled Bush to send troops into Afghanistan (October 2001) and then Iraq in March 2003. The invasion of Iraq led to a deep division in the United States that continued through Bush's reelection in 2004. While many hailed Bush's determination to help the Iraqi people create a democracy, others were convinced it had only provided a breeding ground for terrorists.

The other major decision was a whopping tax cut of $1.35 trillion—by far the largest in history. Critics claimed that the cut benefited the wealthy at the expense of low-income Americans. In addition, it helped to erase the budget surplus of the Clinton years and create the largest annual deficit in history.

Work Out the Numbers

Many Democrats feel that the candidacy of Ralph Nader cost Al Gore the election. The reason: Nader, an environmentalist, took some of the votes of environmentally concerned voters away from Al Gore. Work out the numbers to see how much of a difference Nader's Green (or Independent) Party made. Use the chart on page 119 to answer the following questions.

1 Bush won all 27 electoral votes in Florida. What was his margin of victory over Gore in the popular vote? _____ votes

2 How many of Nader's votes would Gore have needed to carry Florida if we assume that the rest would go to Bush? _____

How many of Nader's votes would Bush have?

a. Gore would need _____.

b. Bush would have _____.

3 Remember, a candidate who wins a state's popular vote wins all of the state's electoral votes. How would the electoral vote change if Gore carried Florida?

Bush: _____

Gore: _____

4 In another close race, in Gore's home state of Tennessee, why would Nader's votes not make a difference? _____

5 Nader's votes in New Hampshire could have given the state's 4 electoral votes to Gore. How would that change the electoral vote? _____

The 2000 Presidential Election Results

National Results

	Popular Vote	Percentage	Electoral Vote
Bush	50,486,167	48	271
Gore	50,996,064	48.5	266
Nader	2,864,810	2.7	

Florida Results

	Popular Vote	Electoral Vote
Bush	2,912,790	27
Gore	2,912,253	0
Nader	97,488	0

Tennessee Results

Bush	1,061,949	11
Gore	981,720	0
Nader	19,781	0

Answers appear at the back of the book.

Separating Names

When Bush became president, there was some confusion about the best way to distinguish the second President George Bush from the first President George Bush. The problem was similar to the other father-son presidents: John Adams and John Quincy Adams. Some refer to the first Bush as the elder Bush or H. W. Bush. One of the most popular solutions is to call the younger Bush by the Texas pronunciation of his middle initial W: Dubya.

Texas Hash

President Bush is a fan of everything Texan, and Texas foods are among his favorites, including this dish that originated in Mexico but has been renamed Texas Hash.

1 Have an adult preheat the oven to 350 degrees F.

2 Melt the butter in a skillet, and slowly cook the onion and pepper until soft. Stir frequently.

3 Add the ground beef and brown it until it is thoroughly cooked. Stir frequently.

4 Lightly grease the casserole dish. Add the meat, onion, and pepper, then the can of tomatoes, rice, water, chili powder, cumin, oregano, salt, and pepper. Stir to combine.

5 Bake at 350 F degrees for 1 hour.

6 Have an adult helper use oven mitts to remove the casserole from the oven. Allow it to cool for 20 minutes. Serve warm.

The advance of liberty is the path to both a safer and better world.

Things You'll Need

2 tablespoons butter
2 cups chopped onion
¾ cup chopped green pepper
1 pound lean ground beef
one 14½-ounce can diced tomatoes
½ cup uncooked rice
½ cup water
½ teaspoon chili powder
¼ teaspoon cumin
¼ teaspoon oregano
1 teaspoon salt
pepper
adult helper
measuring cup
measuring spoon
cutting board
paring knife
large, deep skillet
wooden spoon
2-quart casserole dish
oven mitts
MAKES 4 SERVINGS

ANSWERS

George Washington

1. GENERAL
2. MOUNT VERNON
3. MILITIA
4. INDIANS
5. SURVEYOR
6. BATTLE
7. CONTINENTAL
8. REVOLUTION
9. INDEPENDENCE
10. E T I D S E N R P = PRESIDENT

Thomas Jefferson

1. 775,000
2. the Louisiana Territory; 53,000 square miles
3. 1,603,000 square miles

James Madison

1. James Monroe
2. James Madison
3. Andrew Jackson
4. Martin Van Buren
5. William Henry Harrison
6. John Adams
7. John Quincy Adams
8. Thomas Jefferson

9. George Washington
10. John Tyler

James Monroe

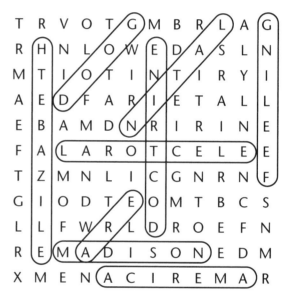

Martin Van Buren

POLK
ADAMS
JACKSON
LINCOLN
WASHINGTON
JEFFERSON
MADISON
MONROE
HARRISON
P D S I T E N E R = PRESIDENT

William Henry Harrison

President's Name	Year Elected	Year Died
Lincoln	1860	1865
McKinley	1900	1901
Harding	1920	1923
Franklin D. Roosevelt (third term)	1940	1945
John F. Kennedy	1960	1963

President Who Broke the "Curse"

Reagan	1980	2004

John Tyler

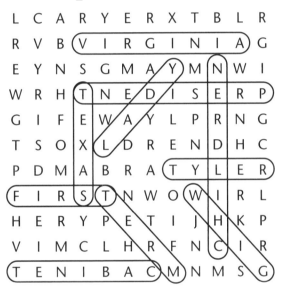

Zachary Taylor

VA**Q**UEROS
B**L**ACK HAWK
VICTORY
P**O**LK
ROUGH
U**N**IFORM
SOLDIER
M**E**XICO
TA**Y**LOR
MARGARET
SERA**P**E
UNION
ZACHARY
SANT**A** ANNA
WAR

Millard Fillmore

C**A**YUGA
ELECT
A**B**IGAIL
JAPAN
WHI**G**
BU**F**FALO
HOUSE
KNOW
NOT**H**ING
IN**D**ENTURED
CAROLINE

James Buchanan

Abraham Lincoln

1. SKILL   2. VOTES   3. CABIN   4. HOUSE

5. SLAVE   6. STORE   7. SOUTH   8. UNION

Last column: V L I C I R W A = CIVIL WAR

121

James A. Garfield

Solution: GARFIELD is spelled from right to left beginning 5 rows from the top and 4 columns from the right.

Grover Cleveland

1. GOVE**R**NOR
2. PRESIDE**NT**
3. H**A**RRISON
4. WHIT**E** HOUSE
5. **S**HERIFF
6. BU**FF**ALO
7. **C**LEVELAND
8. R N A E S F C = FRANCES

Theodore Roosevelt

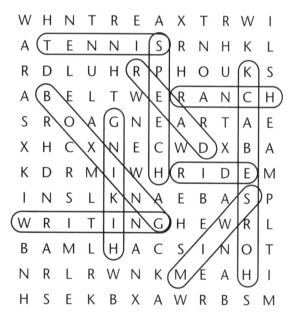

William Howard Taft

1. WILD
2. DROPPED
3. CATCH
4. PITCH

5. LINE
6. ONE
7. STEAL
8. HEEL

Famous Quote:

"THE LONELIEST PLACE IN THE WORLD."

Woodrow Wilson

New Countries	Middle East (mandates)
Finland	Syria (Fr.)
Estonia	Cyprus (Br.)
Latvia	Lebanon (Fr.)
Lithuania	Palestine (Br.)
Poland	Trans-Jordan (Br.)
Austria	Egypt (Br.)
Hungary	
Yugoslavia	
Czechoslovakia	
Bessarabia	

Warren Gamaliel Harding

1. PARTY
2. SPEAK
3. YACHT
4. WHITE
5. ELECT
6. COURT
7. HOUND
8. POKER
9. SHIPS
10. TRAIN

P M O A D E T T O E = TEAPOT DOME

Franklin Delano Roosevelt

1. **D**EPRESSION
2. **LE**GS
3. DELA**N**O
4. N**A**VY
5. **W**AR
6. SENAT**E**
7. E**L**ECTION
8. D E N A W E L = NEW DEAL

John Fitzgerald Kennedy

The missing letter is "A."

1. J<u>A</u>CK
2. R<u>A</u>CE
3. BO<u>A</u>T
4. N<u>A</u>VY
5. B<u>A</u>CK
6. CUB<u>A</u>

Richard Milhous Nixon

Gerald Rudolph Ford

1. NAVAL
2. VETO
3. HOUSE
4. ATHLETE
5. MIGHT
6. REGION
7. IRON
8. RAN

"OUR LONG NATIONAL NIGHTMARE IS OVER."

Bill Clinton

1. TERMS   N
2. WHITE   J
3. WATER   H
4. HOUSE   N
5. ELECT   O
6. VOTER   O
7. PEACE   S
8. N J H N O O S = JOHNSON

George Walker Bush

1. 537
2. Gore would need 49,281. Bush would have 48,207. The margin would still be 537.
3. Bush: 244 (he would lose Florida's 27); Gore: 293
4. Gore would still lose by more than 60,000 votes.
5. Bush would have 267; Gore would have 270.

INDEX